BRINGING HYGGE INTO THE EARLY YEARS

Bringing Hygge into the Early Years is a "how-to" guide for every early educator who wishes to bring more calmness and balance into their day, in turn, leaving them feeling empowered to teach and live well.

Drawing from the author's experience of embracing the Scandinavian way of living well, "hygge", this book explores how this approach can have a positive impact across your early years setting, from improved mental health and wellbeing, to embracing child-led play and high-quality outdoor provision. With step-by-step guidance on how to embed the approach alongside examples of hygge from early educators around the world, the book is divided into four main parts:

- Re-balance you
- The hygge environment
- Slow teaching
- Embracing nature

Throughout each chapter, case studies and activities provide the opportunity to reflect on existing practice and support you as you make positive changes to both your wellbeing and provision. This guide will be essential reading for all early years professionals, offering further support to improve mental health and wellbeing, as well as valuable tools to lead early years practice with confidence and joy.

Kimberly Smith has a passion for child-led, nature-based learning and has worked in Early Years Education for the last 17 years as an early years teacher, leader and trainer. She has worked for the local authority in the quality improvement team, guest lectured at Trinity College London and the University of Leeds, UK, and is a regular conference speaker. Kimberly is now the founder of KSEY Consultancy, working with tens of thousands of educators around the world, to improve their wellbeing and quality of teaching.

"We desperately need teaching to join the Slow Movement, for both educators' and children's wellbeing, happiness and love of learning. Kimberly's wise, practical and supportive advice is so timely, providing great coverage of the many elements of calming things down and enjoying them more in educational settings.

Discovering what calmness looks like for you and your children will transform the way you support learning – your children need you to read and use this book."

Professor Jan White, *Educational consultant, author and advocate for an early childhood outdoors*

"A rich and comprehensive guide to the joyful calm of hygge – each page seems to glow with a simple warmth and the whole book just feels like we are on a walk with Kimberly as she shares her wisdom and a treasure of practical ideas. It's a walk that's very much needed, both for ourselves as practitioners and the children we have the privilege to work with. We all need more hygge in life and Kimberly shows us how just perfectly."

Greg Botrill, *Author and childhood advocate*

BRINGING HYGGE INTO THE EARLY YEARS

A STEP-BY-STEP GUIDE TO BRING A CALM AND SLOW APPROACH TO YOUR TEACHING

Kimberly Smith

LONDON AND NEW YORK

Cover image: Kimberly Smith and Getty Images

First published 2022
by Routledge
2 Park Square, Milton Park, Abingdon, Oxon OX14 4RN

and by Routledge
605 Third Avenue, New York, NY 10158

Routledge is an imprint of the Taylor & Francis Group, an informa business

British Library Cataloguing-in-Publication Data
A catalogue record for this book is available from the British Library

Library of Congress Cataloging-in-Publication Data
Names: Smith, Kimberly, 1986- author.
Title: Bringing hygge into the early years : a step-by-step guide to bring a calm and slow approach to your teaching / Kimberly Smith.
Description: Abingdon, Oxon ; New York, NY : Routledge, 2022. | Includes bibliographical references and index.
Identifiers: LCCN 2021040220 (print) | LCCN 2021040221 (ebook) | ISBN 9781032039626 (hardback) | ISBN 9781032039619 (paperback) | ISBN 9781003189954 (ebook)
Subjects: LCSH: Early childhood educators--Mental health. | Early childhood education--Psychological aspects. | Reflective teaching.
Classification: LCC LB1775.6 .S65 2022 (print) | LCC LB1775.6 (ebook) | DDC 372.21--dc23
LC record available at https://lccn.loc.gov/2021040220
LC ebook record available at https://lccn.loc.gov/2021040221

ISBN: 978-1-032-03962-6 (hbk)
ISBN: 978-1-032-03961-9 (pbk)
ISBN: 978-1-003-18995-4 (ebk)

DOI: 10.4324/9781003189954

Typeset in DIN Pro
by Deanta Global Publishing Services, Chennai, India

CONTENTS

ACKNOWLEDGEMENTS

The foundations of this book were created based upon my journey of discovering "hygge" and the impact embracing it had on both my personal and professional life. Although there are so many wonderful people that have made this book possible through the sharing of their own personal stories and in the process of writing it has indeed turned into "our" book. This book would not have been possible without the collaborative working of my many members on the Hygge in the Early Years Accreditation who have shared such honest reflections of their work in early education and I'm very proud of all that they have achieved personally and professionally.

I would lastly like to thank Professor Jan White, Greg Botrill and Jessica Joelle Alexander for their support and encouragement in putting this book together.

INTRODUCTION

My name's Kimberly and I'm a lover of spending time in nature and finding joy in seasonal living. I'm an early years teacher, leader and founder of the Hygge in the Early Years™ movement. I have written this book along with my signature training course "The Hygge in the Early Years™ Accreditation" to help you become the creator of a calmer and happier approach to your teaching and personal life. I will be sharing with you my personal story of how I went from being an overworked anxiety-ridden educator to leading with calmness, confidence and joy. I have gone on to support tens of thousands of educators as they build a happier and calmer life too and I can't wait to share their life-changing journeys with you.

In the early days of my teaching career everything used to be at such a fast pace, rushing from one activity to the next, never getting to know the children, having a daily lunch date with the laminator and creating provision that ticked a box but didn't actually meet the children's needs. I used to spend so much time in the evenings doing paperwork that had no impact on the children, and this was all fuelled with sugary snacks and coffee. I found that I was missing out on special moments with family and friends yet never reached the end of my to-do list. I realised that as a member of staff I could quickly be replaced but being there for precious moments with my loved ones was something only I could do. It left me feeling drained, anxious and fed up. When Sunday afternoons arrived, I would feel a familiar tightening in my chest at the thought of the week ahead. I wonder if you can relate to this?

For me, everything changed when I discovered the Danish secret to improved wellbeing and happiness – hygge. This happened during a summer holiday travelling around Scandinavia with my Norwegian friend and staying with her family.

Hygge (pronounced hue-guh) is a Danish concept that cannot be translated to one single word but encompasses a feeling of cosy contentment and wellbeing by enjoying the simple things in life. For example, taking the time to appreciate the first cup of coffee on a morning before anyone else gets up, a snowy walk through the woods and feeling the freshness of the cold on your skin, or getting together with loved ones for a shared meal around the dining table.

DOI: 10.4324/9781003189954-1

Learning about hygge naturally encourages you to slow down and be present in the current moment. This allows you to really feel appreciation for all that you have each day, bringing in the emotional impact of increased calm, peace and contentment and leaving hygge as one of the main contributors to Denmark being voted as one of the happiest nations year on year in the World Happiness Report.

During my time in Scandinavia, I loved how every day was celebrated and I began to see that life wasn't something you squeezed in time for around a busy day at work. Instead, the day involved living life well and tuning into the simple moments that would bring joy – and then planning more of this. Prior to this as a teacher I would always count down the days till the weekend or my next holiday and would dedicate my evenings and Sundays to doing more work. This meant that I saved up all the best moments of my life for a later time, never living in the present moment and almost wishing my life away. I worked out that living for the next weekend meant wishing away 71% of the week. I learnt that you have to change your mindset and not save lighting your favourite candle for winter, using your best dinner plates for a special occasion or seeing your friends just for a weekend. Live your life today because this day is special and unique and won't ever happen again.

I also realised that the way we organise our homes and the atmosphere we create here can have an impact on our wellbeing and help us feel calmer. Cosy areas to sit and read were created, the interiors were all clutter-free and decorated in neutral décor and furnished with warm textures. I liked the way nature was embraced inside and how the joys of each season were celebrated.

After my adventures around Scandinavia, I reflected on what I had learnt and started to make some changes to my personal life by embracing the slower way of living. This involved sitting down in the morning and having a good healthy breakfast before leaving for work, embracing daily time in nature, and no longer working on evenings and weekends. I soon began to feel the impact of these small changes and realised that when I invested in my own self-care I had more to give back to those around me. I wondered why this had never been covered in my teacher training? I began to question, if I could make these changes in my personal life then could I also apply the hygge concept into the way I taught? I thought about the current education system and wondered if it was outdated; if what today's children needed was something different than what had been in place since the industrial revolution.

The outbreak of COVID-19 and the world pandemic has taught us that no amount of knowledge helps us to overcome challenges like this. Instead, we need to have a collection of tools and strategies that we can turn to that support our own mental health when moments in life get tough or feel unknown. To know how to show up and respond with a growth mindset, courage, perseverance, resilience, strength, bravery and hope. For me hygge is one of those tools.

In a world that seems to be getting faster, busier and more frantic perhaps there is an even greater need for schools and settings to increase their levels of calmness while fostering comfort and togetherness. Time moves so quickly and we often feel ourselves caught up in the race to get to the next thing when actually we need space in our day to value the preciousness of having a childhood; this is not something to be rushed through.

I took these thoughts back to my team and we began to make changes to our provision, organising the clutter, calming it down by adding rugs and plants, and generally creating a space that felt more homely. Setting up cosy nooks to sit and talk in and adding beautiful prints and decorations instead of getting a headache from all the shiny laminated signs acting as wallpaper that had previously been there.

We made changes to our daily routine and slowed everything down. Tweaking our planning to make it more relevant and responsive to the children's fascinations and interests. Gone were my weekends of sitting at a computer typing up a forward plan for something that might never happen. I was getting my time back and had more freedom with my day. I didn't have to turn down a family BBQ on a Sunday afternoon anymore.

These changes all made a massive impact on the relationships I formed with the children, their levels of engagement and involvement during play and also the way we equipped them to be lifelong learners.

Fast forward ten years and I've not only transformed my own practice and led my team through two outstanding inspections but I've also been able to make a life-changing impact on the tens of thousands of educators I've worked with on my training courses.

I've helped early educators re-claim their time and create precious moments with their family, while also being highly successful in their jobs.

Take Nicola as an example. She inherited a cluttered, chaotic environment that was overbearing on the senses. After taking part in my training her team have transformed the space to create flexible provision areas with a beautiful dining table for children to eat lunch together as a family.

Or how about Robert? He was feeling like his team were drowning in paperwork, which was taking their time away from the children. As a result of my training, he's slowed the planning down and made it more around the child's needs. Now he reports his team want to come to work, there are fewer staff sick days, they take ownership for the learning and resources and feel excited for the day ahead. Robert said he was so happy to finally find a human and caring approach to early education.

Then there was Sarah, who was at breaking point in her teaching career. Then she discovered my training and it literally changed her life. She started to put her own self-care and wellbeing first and found that this gave her more to give back to those around her.

To successfully embrace hygge you have to do something you've never done before. The changes needed might take you out of your comfort zone to begin with as it involves doing something different when you've always done it a certain way.

But if you're wanting to feel better you have to do something different to what you've always done. If you're wanting big changes in your practice then you're going to need guidance from someone that's done it. I would love it if that someone could be me. If you're needing inspiration for your practice and would like to teach and live well then I can show you their experiences as their stories are woven through the book.

During the Part 1 of this book, we're going to take some time to unpick exactly what hygge is to you and the impact it can have on your wellbeing and mental health. There will be links to other wellbeing approaches around the world that can also inspire living well. We will explore how to cultivate more happiness in your day with the five pillars of happiness, reduce stress and the feelings of burnout and discover ways to be more efficient with your time. These strategies will become the foundational pieces of your approach to life as you discover how investing more time in you will lead to greater success in all aspects of your life.

By the end of Part 2 you will have learnt how easy it is to bring the hygge atmosphere into your setting to create purposeful and calm provision, leading to higher levels of engagement and empowering you to make an impact, leaving you and your children feeling calmer and ready to learn.

During Part 3 we will continue to build on embracing hygge in your early years practice by slowing down your day and going with child-led planning. We will explore ways you can reduce unnecessary paperwork and plan your day so that it has the greatest impact on your learners, taking time to explore the difference between a provocation and an invitation to play and responding to the unique needs of each child even when you have a reception class of 30!

By the time you finish Part 4, our final section together, you will be excited and inspired to take learning into the outdoors no matter what the weather. I will share with you some of the ways you can overcome barriers to getting outside including only having a concrete area, lacking in budget and making learning happen on rainy days!

Lastly, this isn't a book trying to encourage you to adopt an approach where every setting looks the same or simply export the Scandinavian practice you read about and put it directly into your setting. This book should be viewed as a self-discovery for you and your team to explore what joy and calmness looks like for you, the elements you can resonate with and then add it into your own unique practice and culture accordingly. I'm sure there will be parts of this book you will take and blend in with the other successful international perspectives to create a practice that's needed for your children.

If you're ready, let's find out what hygge means to you and discover what lights you up.

Kimberly

PART 1

RE-BALANCE YOU

I remember when I was striving to be a successful early years teacher. I would attend courses, read books and reflect on my teaching daily. Yet none of this had the impact I desired when I didn't have the tools to plan my time effectively, or have the mindset I needed to be positive when I came to my first hurdle. I remember not eating well and fuelling my days with coffee and sugar which then resulted in poor sleep on an evening.

It was when I started to prioritise my mental health and wellbeing that I was able to believe in myself and be an outstanding teacher. I gathered up a collection of daily habits for success and also spent my evenings and weekends with friends and family instead of my life being dominated by work.

This first section of this book is around re-balancing yourself by understanding what your struggles and barriers are and showing just what's possible when you begin to make changes to your day. It will help you to prioritise your own mental health, leading to a positive impact on the children's learning and development, and will highlight success stories and case studies from other early educators along the way to prove just what's possible.

In this section we will focus on:

- Discovering what hygge is
- Unlocking the secrets to improved wellbeing and happiness
- Understanding how you can plan your time more effectively
- Finding strategies to help you feel calmer
- Exploring the link to your core values and your early years practice

DOI: 10.4324/9781003189954-2

Chapter one

HOW HYGGE SUPPORTS YOU

When taking a flight in the event of an emergency we're often reminded of the importance of fitting our own oxygen mask first before helping others with theirs. This same concept can be applied to your teaching: you can't support and inspire others, if you're tired, run down or feeling stressed. One of my members recently told me that she decided to embrace hygge as, "I'm so used to putting everyone else first and never do anything for me. I've forgotten who I am these days and I want to remember who I am and be kind to myself."

Data collected in a major report "Minds Matter" carried out by the Pre-school Learning Alliance (2018) showed that 74% of early educators experienced work-related stress in the month they took part in the study, indicating the extent of mental health challenges faced by the early years sector.

I know what this stress can feel like first-hand as there were times at the start of my career when I worked as an early years teacher and often had feelings of overwhelm and anxiety around doing my job well. I had an ever-growing to-do list and very little time to do these tasks. I would get up early to be the first at work and would always be the last one to leave. My weekends and evenings were often consumed with more work and my social life became non-existent as I was either working or exhausted. The stress of the job was having such a negative impact on the way my body was responding. My skin was dull, my eyes had lost their sparkle (and had been replaced with dark bags), I was exhausted, my body ached and my wellbeing levels were low.

There are many different definitions of wellbeing and it varies slightly around the world. In general, it refers to feeling at ease, being spontaneous and free of emotional tensions and is crucial to good "mental health." It can be linked to self-confidence, a good degree of self-esteem and resilience. NHS England defines stress as "the body's reaction to feeling threatened or under pressure," and although a little bit of stress every now and again can be motivating to get things done, prolonged stress over time can cause burnout, which leaves a negative impact on our bodies:

DOI: 10.4324/9781003189954-3

- **Insomnia:** This includes broken sleep, struggling to fall asleep and nightmares.
- **Muscles aches:** When you feel under pressure, you're unsure of how your leader might react to something and you hold your body so tight with so much tension. This is often felt in the back, neck and shoulders. It may feel like you've been lifting a heavy weight.
- **Dizziness:** When you're stressed, your body produces a surge of hormones which makes your heart beat faster and your blood vessels narrow, which can lead to feelings of being light-headed and feeling dizzy. Longer term this also increases your blood pressure and puts you at a greater risk of a heart attack or stroke.
- **Weakened immune system:** If you're feeling under pressure and stressed then your immune system is weakened. This might mean you catch every bug going around and need to take more sick days, which can then increase the level of stress you feel.
- **Exhaustion:** Do you feel as though it's just too hard to get up in the morning? You press snooze three times; you need a nap mid-afternoon and crave sleep-ins on a weekend? When we find it hard to relax and switch off, our body doesn't have any down time and we end up running on empty.

Feeling stressed is not only having a negative effect on your wellbeing but it can also influence those around you. How many times have you been at work and felt like the children just weren't listening or that your team were pushing all your buttons? Next time you feel this particular way I want you to just stop for two minutes and consider your feelings. Did you have a particularly stressful morning before work or an argument about burnt toast with your partner? We often find that if we are experiencing a bad day or feeling tired then our mood can start to impact those around us. When we take a look at neuroscience, we can understand that the brain loves to imitate, therefore if you're feeling grumpy or excited it can be contagious to those around you. Scientists (Fadiga et al., 1995) understand that imitation functions through a system of mirror neurons. As we watch another person mirror neurons fire through the motor cortex and map that movement into our bodies. This shows us that we need to be the energy we want from others in our classroom and provides another reason to improve your own mental health and wellbeing.

When my member Rachael started to prioritise her wellbeing she began to see a huge impact in her work as well as her personal life. This also involved the acceptance of not being able to do everything and learning how to say no.

> Hygge in the Early Years course has had a massive impact on me and my setting. Unlike any other course, it focused on my wellbeing too, something I never had time for and always felt guilty about. At the start of the course, I was at an all-time low in my career – I needed a major operation, wasn't sleeping and felt stuck in a rut, doing the same routines. The course taught me to prioritise my own wellbeing, to slow things down and not feel guilty about stepping back from commitments and I had always done, like running groups. We now embrace the Hygge aspect "presence" – living in the moment. We go for walks, we sit in woods (and sometimes puddles), we listen to the birds singing or read a book on our walk (all good phonics activities too). We've slowed down. We also have more natural resources (mainly free or home-made), we do yoga and activities are more child led, process over product. The children are more engaged and the pace of the setting is calmer and relaxed. If there's one step I'd recommend, it's take a good look at what you do each week. Is it the same thing purely from routine? Can you step back and do something different? Don't feel guilty about putting your own wellbeing first; you can then be strong enough to support others.
>
> (Rachael Hill, childminder)

Each year The World Happiness Report ranks 156 countries by their happiness levels. In 2020 Finland held the top spot for the third year in a row with Denmark coming in at a close second. Denmark, Switzerland, Norway and Finland have consistently held the top places on the list for the last six years. All four countries tend to have high values for all six of the key variables that have been found to support wellbeing: income, healthy life expectancy, social support, freedom, trust and generosity.

Denmark also has the key to high levels of happiness with its approach to living well – "Hygge."

What is hygge?

Hygge is the Danish approach to living well that focuses on being in the moment and embracing the feelings of warmth, simplicity and connection. The term first appeared in written Danish in the early 1800s and is believed to originate from the word hug. Meik Wiking, author of *The Little Book of Hygge* and founder of the Happiness Research Institute in Copenhagen, believes that there are ten principles that must be considered to live a hygge lifestyle. These are:

- Atmosphere
- Presence
- Pleasure
- Equality
- Togetherness
- Gratitude
- Harmony
- Truce
- Comfort
- Shelter

(Principles taken from Wiking, M. (2016) The Little Book of Hygge)

We can explore hygge in more detail by considering what each principle looks like in practice.

- **Atmosphere:** Creating a calm vibe
- **Presence:** Not being on your phone and living in the moment
- **Pleasure:** It should be fun, enjoyable and bring great happiness
- **Equality:** No one is better than anyone else
- **Togetherness:** Spend time with people you care about and those that make you smile
- **Gratitude:** Take time to reflect on what you're grateful for
- **Harmony:** Life is not a competition
- **Truce:** No need for arguments
- **Comfort:** Relax, wear fluffy socks and be cosy
- **Shelter:** Your home is important

Hygge is a very sensory experience and we can tune into the simple pleasures in life with our senses while also improving our wellbeing. For instance, just looking at something beautiful can make you feel more joy as it releases dopamine. This is the part of our brain responsible for feeling pleasure.

Seeing hygge: It could be a shaft of sunlight hitting the coffee table, the glittering reflections on the sea, a flicker of candlelight, a bird taking a dip in your birdbath or the first snowdrop after a long winter.

Feeling hygge: The comforting weight of a cat sat on your lap, the warmth on your hands from a mug of tea on a chilly afternoon, the feel of the sun on your skin as you relax by a pool, the embrace of a loved one in your arms or a gentle breeze on your skin as you walk along the beach.

Smelling hygge: The aroma of bluebells after a rainstorm, the nostalgic smell of an old English tea rose taking you back to your childhood, your baby that's just been bathed, the smell of baking filling your kitchen or the smell of the rain as it hits dry ground.

Tasting hygge: Freshly baked scones with jam and cream, the slurp of your homemade soup warming your insides or tasting summer in a glass as you drink your freshly squeezed orange juice.

With the long dark nights and harsh winters, the Danes must have a mindset of positivity. Hygge is felt even more when something negative is going on around you. When speaking to a Dane while on my travels they said, "I love closing the curtains at the end of the day when it's dark outside. It signifies cosy time for me by shutting out the outside and busy world." When it's cold and snowing the situation is turned around and they light a fire, gather candles and get comfy under blankets. They take enjoyment from the warmth they experience while reading a book by the fire and watching the snow fall outside. When it's raining it's a chance to use an umbrella they love and it waters their plants. As the darkness comes in it's used as an opportunity to light a fire and toast marshmallows and come together to tell stories as the flames dance. The darkness can offer an opportunity to stargaze as well.

Activity

Discovering what hygge feels like for you will be different to how a colleague experiences it. The individual things that light us up in life make us who we are. Make a hygge scrapbook or vision board of what hygge looks, smells, tastes and feels like to you by gathering a collection of images or quotes that you resonate with. These can then be shared with colleagues and you could develop a collective one for your team.

Activity

Remember that Danes don't live just for the happiness of a next holiday or the weekend but actually live for simple and joyful moments each day. Make a list of everything you enjoy doing then a separate list of what you do each day. Now add something that you love to your daily list.

My hygge day

Hygge feels different for everyone and I wanted to share with you what it feels and looks like for me by telling you about our very hygge Sunday.

We began our morning by having a slow breakfast together as a family where we lit the candles and talked about what we all wanted to do on such a cold foggy day. Despite the weather, we decided to get wrapped up and embrace the great outdoors. We headed out for an autumn walk through the woods and to a nearby dam.

As we walked along we took in the smell of the trees, the oozing of the mud on our boots and the sound of the birds in the trees. We also loved collecting up many natural treasures like pine cones, leaves and stones.

Once we got back from our chilly walk we decided to get warm and cosy by building a hygge den in the living room. We filled our den with warm blankets, twinkly lights and some of our favourite books. As we read the story of the Gingerbread Man and sipped our hot chocolate we could hear the gentle sound of raindrops hitting the velux roof. We loved the repetitive story of the Gingerbread Man and the beautiful illustrations in the book. We used some storytelling cards to help us re-tell the story in our play. It then inspired us to bake our very own delicious gingerbread as well and the house was filled with the sweet aroma of our baking.

At the end of our afternoon we returned back to the children's interests from the woodland walk and used a batch of natural playdough to explore leaves. This was a very calming way to end such a hyggelig day.

Sometimes we feel as though our day isn't going to plan or we might be feeling tired. To introduce hygge into your routine when you feel it hasn't been a good day it might look like this:

At the end of a busy morning session in nursery I made time to have my lunch, reminding myself that doing this isn't an act of wellbeing but is actually an essential part of my day. I sat in our outdoor area to eat and when I'd finished I applied some relaxing hand cream and took two minutes to do some deep breathing. At the end of my working day I got into the car and put my favourite feel-good playlist on. As I arrived home I made myself a nice mug of hot tea and dipped a biscuit in it as I reflected on the day. These few quiet moments to myself are always key for reflection and winding down from a hectic day. We then made a family dinner together and sat around the table chatting as we ate. After dinner we spent some time in the garden watering our plants (which is always very soothing on the senses) and feeding the chickens before taking a shower with calming essential oils and getting into bed.

Activity

Try a piece of creative writing about what your own version of a hygge day would look and feel like.

Approaching wellbeing around the world

Many Danes believe that hygge can only be practised in Denmark but I think there are elements we can take from this approach to happiness and feel inspired by. We can also look around the world at what other countries are doing to support wellbeing.

In Japan their concept of Ikigai is all about discovering your purpose in life and how this can match up to your values and what you enjoy. This gives you a reason to get up in the morning and also helps you to live longer. There is also Japanese Kintsugi which offers a very useful life lesson that nothing is ever truly broken. Here fractured pottery is fixed with gold. The practice of Shinrin Yoku, which translates as forest bathing, also developed in Japan in the 1980s as a preventative health care method and is based on the belief that there are physical and mental benefits from spending time soaking in the atmosphere of a forest. Studies by Furuyashiki et al. (2019) have shown that spending just 15 minutes walking between the trees can reduce blood pressure, lower stress levels and help with the clarity of your thinking.

In 2017 New Zealand made the headlines around the world as they announced their wellbeing budget. The government focused on prioritising mental wellbeing, showing that financial growth was not the only indicator of a country's progress. All government spending was linked to how it supported the five specific wellbeing goals: bolstering mental health, reducing child poverty, supporting indigenous peoples, moving to a low-carbon-emission economy and flourishing in a digital age.

Over in Mumbai, India in 1995, Dr Madan Kataria's article titled "Laughter – the Best Medicine" highlighted through her research that laughter can be combined with movements like yoga to have a huge emotional and physical impact on mental health and wellbeing.

Taking an international look at wellbeing shows us that we don't just have to stick to one singular approach to supporting our own wellbeing. Instead we can mix and match what is most effective for us and use elements of each to help discover our calm.

Chapter two

MANAGING YOUR TIME

Do you half run into work? Are you often eating on the go as it allows you to multitask? Is this hamster wheel of hecticness driving you crazy each and every day? There is often a notion that being "busy" equates to being more successful in life. Yet the Danes believe the opposite of this and, rather, being busy shows that you're inefficient at how you use the time that's given. Perhaps you're feeling time-poor and haven't been successful at getting things done today, or you've been too busy to even have a sip of water all day. Yet looking at your phone and the amount of time you've spent on it tells a different story. We all have time but it's up to us how we choose to spend it.

During my travels in Scandinavia, I was surprised to see rush hour begins between 3 and 4 pm in the afternoon. This allows the Danes to get home in good time to spend the evenings with their family, cooking a meal together or doing hobbies. By switching off from work on an evening they can be more energised and productive once they return the next day. They still work hard during their 37-hour official working week but they understand that there needs to be a balance between work and home. As much as you may enjoy your job, work is not life but if you let it then it can take over. In Denmark, full-time workers spend on average 66% of their day working on their self-care and taking part in leisure activities.

Embracing a day full of slow moments might mean you have to re-think how you currently spend your time.

Activity: Not-to-do list

You might be feeling resentful of your job at the moment as it robs you of your time and leaves you with nothing to give back to your family and friends. We all crave more freedom in the way we spend our days. One of the biggest things we need to focus on here when re-claiming our time is to consider what we're doing in our day that's having the most impact on our goals.

DOI: 10.4324/9781003189954-4

Daily Routine (The activities I do on an average day/week)	Time Spent On It	How It Makes You Feel	Does It Have Impact?

If we're finding our days are filled with moments that have no impact we can reflect on how we can do less of these activities. It should hopefully give you the confidence to say no to doing these or delegate them to a more suitable or appropriate member of the team. Also consider who you're spending your time with and ask yourself are they draining you of your positive energy? It might be as a childminder that you attend a group on a Tuesday morning but feel it's become more of a complaining session than a positive experience.

What are the three activities that have the most positive impact on your day?

1.

2.

3.

What are the activities that have the least positive impact on your day and what can you do to change this?

1.

2.

3.

Activity: Your priority list

After losing the activities in our day/week that are moving the impact needle the least we can then make sure we are efficient with getting the tasks done that are required. We can become really clear on the actions we need to take and add a sense of calmness each day by writing a priority list. I like to choose 3–4 actions each day to include on here of things I must get done. I then write these in order of priority with 1 being most urgent to do and I consider how much time is needed in my day to achieve it.

With every action you put on your priority list I want you to get into the habit of asking yourself the following questions:

- What's my why for needing to do it?
- What do I really want to accomplish?
- How is this going to have impact?

Chapter three

BECOMING PRESENT

As the world gets faster, busier and more instant we can lose track of appreciating what we have right now. Working flat out and struggling to switch off and relax isn't good for you or your teaching. Urgency was once saved for a one-off deadline or special occasion but now it's an everyday occurrence. We all need time to stop and reflect, to regain our perspective and take stock of our tasks. We can be good at taking care of our physical health with a good diet and exercise but it's important we feed our hearts and mind too. However, stopping and not feeling guilty for doing this is easier said than done. My member Heather realised that her life as a teacher and a childminder used to be just focused on surviving the day.

> Before I discovered hygge I always felt stressed and overworked with no time for myself or family and friends. My work life as a teacher and now childminder completely took over and I was so busy that I wasn't actually living my life. I was just surviving. Hygge has totally transformed my world and I'm so much happier now. I've discovered that I love to be in nature and I've regained my home by creating a space that is cosy and inviting rather than like a school classroom. Learning about hygge has given me the confidence to slow learning down, which has had an amazing effect on both mine and the children's wellbeing. I have learnt how to use light, mirrors, and nature to create enchanting provision and to bring excitement to the children's play. I love creating cosy little spaces for the children to curl up with a favourite book and small worlds for the children to lose themselves in their imaginations! Hygge is having such a positive impact on my life, my family's life, and the lives of the children I care for. Hygge will always be part of my life now. I just wish I'd discovered it earlier!
>
> (Heather Gibson)

DOI: 10.4324/9781003189954-5

Wanderlust Child Nature Study
Wildflower Spotter Sheet

slow down
BRING CALM TO A BUSY WORLD WITH 50 NATURE STORIES
In a Garden
Nature Shelf
BUG HOTEL

Mole didn't think
twice. He scurried up and
down the ladders, collecting the
stars one by one, and carrying
them home.

Illustrated
Nursery
Rhymes

Little house on the green childcare

In order to feel hygge we need to be living in this moment now by noticing the world around us. Author Jessica Joelle Alexander (2016) expressed that, "It takes awareness and conscious effort to create hygge for non-Danes, but the results can be magnificent."

It also takes an effort to re-think the way we live in the moment and for Danes they don't define their happiness with materialistic stuff like getting a new car or an expensive watch. Instead they try and create an everyday attitude towards life and avoid chasing after something that will only ever give temporary happiness. Here we can turn to young children and learn from them that it's the simple moments that bring the true happiness. For example, the complete joy they have when jumping in a puddle on a rainy day or creating a story with a cardboard box. We don't have to teach children hygge, all we need to do is give them our time. They will be the ones to dawdle on the way to the shops and be fascinated at the wildflower while you're rushing to achieve the next thing.

Living in the present and not the past or the future is known as mindfulness and this is key to having good mental wellbeing. Professor Mark Williams, former director of the Oxford Mindfulness Centre, describes it as taking the time to know what is directly happening around us and in ourselves. You know that you're living truly in the moment when you can feel the breeze on your face, you see the buds on the tree you walk past and actually listen to what your friend is telling you rather than thinking of the items on your to-do list.

I'm going to give you an example of one of my present moments. We were in Alberta, Canada and we had a wonderful snowshoe walk through the forest. As we walked along I noticed a bird that was following us with lots of white fluffy hair, I could hear the crunch of the snow under my feet and I could see the warmth of my breath in the –10 degree air. There was no-where else I needed to be.

For Danes hygge moments can happen anywhere and at any time. It can be waking up slowly and having breakfast with the family. Taking their time over their meal, chatting about the day ahead and even lighting a candle. This is a time to be enjoyed and not rushed and there is a belief that how you start your day sets you up for the rest of it. Sip your coffee slowly, open the windows to let in a breeze in and enjoy this time of connection. It might then be followed with a morning walk into nature to visit a place of water. Often Danes will enjoy a morning swim outdoors (all year round!) or a forage for shells and sea glass that can be added to the home. Time is taken for consciously making memories. We can all tune into meaningful moments for ourselves in the present.

Being present on a day at work might involve just taking a moment to stand back and watch the extraordinary moment of the children learning and discovering without feeling the need to write anything down. Hearing the way the children connect new ideas together and feeling warm inside as you watch the joy they get from taking part in the magic of their play. For my member Vicki Murray it's joining in with the moment and being barefoot in the mud.

For Early Years Foundation Stage leader Amy, her practice has seen her become even more tuned into the seasonal changes and using these as a way to connect with the present.

> We were already very child-led and planning "in the moment" centred much of what we did, however, the Accreditation has been a valuable opportunity to really reflect on why we do what we do and how we can continually improve. Alongside completing the Wanderlust Nature Study, we now base much of our curriculum in Nursery around nature and the seasons changing around us. We now have weekly visits to our on-site Secret Garden and are encouraging the children to notice the seasonal changes around them.
>
> It has also changed my practise as a leader considering not just my wellbeing and work life balance but that of my whole team. I am appreciating the opportunity to think about what is really important for our children's needs while maintaining a manageable workload. It's not always easy and the pressures of daily school life can still sometimes feel overwhelming but I feel much more prepared to meet these challenges and balance it out with the time I need to be me. Often this "time out" gives me the brain space to then solve problems which before I felt were too much. Giving myself permission to slow down has really made a positive difference.
>
> I'm really glad that I made the decision to make Hygge in the Early Years both part of our daily practice in school and also my life at home.
>
> (Amy Parker, EYFS lead and nursery teacher,
> Prince Edward Primary School, Sheffield)

We explored
orange

Activity

Take some time to consider when you were last truly present and living in the moment. Write down how this made you feel.

Now I know that it can be hard to actually stop our head from swirling with thoughts at times. Breathing is a lovely part of our day which we don't often think about but when we feel stressed or anxious our body takes shorter and more shallow breaths. Box breathing is a very powerful yet simple exercise that we can do anywhere. It's a relaxation technique that aims to return breathing to its normal rhythm and re-balance the nervous system. It can help to clear the mind, relax the body and improve focus.

Activity: Box breathing

Next time you feel anxious give box breathing a go. Breathe in through your nose while counting to four slowly. Feel the air enter your lungs. Hold your breath inside while counting slowly to four. Hold your breath and count to four slowly. Repeat these steps at least five times or until you feel calmer again.

Activity: Body scan

Do you ever find yourself starting to worry about something that's going to happen in the future? Then you're going to find this relaxation exercise really helpful. I'm going to walk you through how you can do a body scan now. This is great for relieving any tension in your muscles and calming your mind down. It can be done alongside a yoga practice as well.

While sitting or lying down on your bed take a few slow and deep breaths in and out. Take time to notice where you can feel the breath in your body. Then starting with your toes, focus your attention on one part of your body at a time. Pay attention to how that area is feeling and notice any sensations that you are experiencing. After a few moments of focused attention, move up to the next part of your body (i.e., after your toes, focus on your feet, then ankles, etc.).

We are reminded by author Matt Haig of how little time it can take to practice mindfulness, "Wherever you are, at any moment, try and find something beautiful. A face, a line out of a poem, the clouds out of a window, some graffiti, a wind farm. Beauty cleans the mind." Here are some quick ideas of ways you can work on being more present even if you feel short of time. They can be planned into your day to help you unwind:

- Lunch outside
- Five slow deep breaths in and out
- Light a candle at mealtimes
- Water your plants
- Walk the dog
- Wash your face
- Apply a hand cream and give yourself a hand massage
- Add some movement into your day; some yoga stretches or jumping jacks
- Spend time in nature
- Colour in a page of a colouring book or do a doodle
- Drink a herbal tea
- Listen to the birds
- Drink a glass of water
- Flick through a magazine
- Journal your thoughts
- Open the window
- Play your favourite song
- Read a chapter of a book

Often there are times in the day where we could be having downtime but instead we find ourselves reaching for our phones because we become worried about missing something. We don't have to be connected to our job 24/7. In France a law was passed in 2017 for workers to disconnect from checking their work emails out of work time and it's known as the Right to Disconnect.

Here are some helpful suggestions of how you can reduce your screen time:

- Set up automations for your emails that allow you to have an evening and weekend off
- Turn off the red notifications that pop up on the apps on your phone
- Use your device in a positive way to listen to a sleep cast or a visualisation
- Give yourself the challenge of using your device to take a daily photo of something that's brought you joy

Thinking for the now

Lastly when it comes to thinking about being present, it's easy to live your life in the past or future and think you were or you would be happier then. Or perhaps you're letting the worry of a week ahead rob you from your Sunday. We need to try and think about the past in small pieces of reflection and consider the "why" of it being on our mind. When thinking about the future in small doses make sure you have a healthy focus. For example, set yourself a short amount of time to think about the anxieties you might have about something but use it as a chance to come up with a plan.

Bring more positivity

When it comes to bringing more positivity to the day I often felt like my negative doubts turned me into my own worst critic. We put so much pressure on ourselves to be the best, to be number one and to be in competition with the world and even those close to us. The messages that we tell ourselves can have a big impact on the mindset we feel. One strategy that I've found to be successful here is the use of daily affirmations and these can be said out loud when needed as well as recorded down on paper in a journal.

Affirmations are the positive messages you tell yourself out loud to eliminate self-doubt. Our subconscious mind doesn't know the difference between past and future or what's happened and what's not. If you repeatedly tell yourself that you're strong, confident and happy then you're going to start believing it. The way we word these messages to our brain is important too. "I am healthy and energetic" instead of "I want to be healthy and energetic" otherwise your brain starts to ask how and why.

Activity

Take a look at the examples of affirmations and consider which you could use in your day.

- I'm not perfect. I am human
- I will be the best that I can be and feel proud
- I never give up
- I am resilient and I am capable to tackle the self-doubt I sometimes face
- I am strong and healthy, I have the energy I need
- There are so many beautiful reasons to be happy
- I am calm and have a calm environment around me
- I believe in myself and my ability
- I make the best of every situation
- I am strong

"Happiness is not an accident, it's something we have to actively choose" (Robson 2010). We can create happy habits in the brain by drawing upon the aspects of life that have the greatest impact on positivity. These can be defined as the five pillars of happiness:

- Mindfulness
- Gratitude
- Journaling
- Act of kindness
- Movement

Mindfulness with children

My member childminder Lynne Fairhurst decided to work with children on being present in each season. They picked a tree that was outside their setting and decided to document the changes to it as they passed through the year. Helping her children to tune into the moment of now. Here are some other ideas of how you could invite your children to have a few mindful moments:

1. Listen to a Tibetan singing bowl
2. Check the daily weather report
3. Imagine you're blowing up a balloon to promote deep breathing
4. Lay on your back with a bean bag on your tummy and slowly breathe to make it move up and down
5. Eat slowly and seasonally and talk about the food together: texture, taste, smell
6. Share some mindful books together, such as *Tiny, Perfect Things* by M. Clark
7. Lay on your back and look up at the clouds and talk about the shapes you see
8. Try a guided visualisation together

Activity

As a group of staff or with your children sit somewhere where you can be comfortable, close your eyes or soften them. Read out the following visualisation slowly and encourage those that you're with to imagine it in their mind.

> Take a moment to get comfortable as we're about to go on a peaceful walk through the snowy forest. Take some slow deep breaths in and out and clear your mind of any other thoughts. There is nowhere else you need to be. Starting at your toes relax your muscles, release the muscles in your legs. Feel your back relaxed and making contact with the chair or floor as it sinks in. Let your stomach relax out and drop your shoulders. Next move your tongue away from the roof of your mouth and gently make the edges of your lips smile. Continue to take slow deep breaths as you imagine the picture I describe in your mind.
>
> Imagine that it's wintertime and you're following a path through a snow-covered peaceful forest. As you walk along you can hear the crunch of the compact snow under your boots. You stop to look around you and can see that

the sunlight catching the snow and it makes everything sparkle. The snow is also balancing carefully on the bare branches of the trees and you notice a little bird is also perched there. There are some fir trees too and as you walk past these your leg brushes them softly. The sky above you is starting to turn grey again and you wonder if there might be more snowfall. You follow the path through the forest and it leads you back to your home. You live in a small wooden cabin in the heart of the woods. You take your key out of your pocket and unlock the door to let yourself in. As soon as you get inside the warmth embraces you like a big hug. You take off your coat and boots and replace these with some soft fluffy slippers. Next you take some off-cuts of wood and put these onto your fire. You stand and watch as the flames from the fire dance around and you hear the crackles. You then make yourself a mug of hot chocolate and take a seat next to the fire. As you sit there slowly sipping your drink you notice that the snow is falling heavily again outside. Take a few deep breaths in and out. Then slowly open your eyes.

Gratitude

The act of gratitude in positive psychology is about taking the time to appreciate what we have to be grateful for now. It's not just the big things or the significant moments in life but the practice of seeing the everyday moments. Often we're in such a rush to find happiness in the next thing that we forget to pause and find the happiness in the now. My member Emma Thackley often takes the time in her day to pause with the children. Perhaps you're thinking that when you get your new phone you'll be happier then. Yet if we can't see the gratitude of what we've already got what makes us believe we'll be grateful if we have more?

Studies by psychologists and mental health researchers (Seligman et al., 2005). shows us that when we take the time for regular gratitude, we are less stressed, have better sleep and improved vitality. Making gratitude an alternative prescription for anti-depressants and a powerful tool that when we do it regularly it can help us find light and positivity even during the darkest times.

Gratitude can take a few different forms:

- It can be the messages your inner voice gives and the way you speak to yourself
- It could be having a gratitude journal and setting aside a time each day to work on it
- A thank you card or letter to someone

You could even try an act of gratitude with your children by lighting a candle each morning and asking what they're grateful for. Writing this onto a tree cookie and hanging it onto an indoor branch tree. At Danish garden kindergarten, Nokken, acts of gratitude are built into the daily routine. For example children will sing the "thanks for the food song" at dinner time and talk about what they've enjoyed. The staff here are also reminded regularly about being grateful for the job they do and that the parents place great trust in the team each day to do the very best for the child.

We can also bring gratitude and positivity into our staffroom and my member Mel Hart and her team at Albion House Nursery have created a positivity board.

> The accreditation has allowed us to take time for ourselves and reflect on our wellbeing. Being a small nursery we are more like a family, and the Danish way of thinking has allowed us to really look out for each other and appreciate each other. We have started a Positivity Wall which allows staff to complement each other on good practice, giving everyone a sense of gratitude when they see a note for them. We believe that where there is a happy staff team the atmosphere and the children are happy too.
>
> We have noticed the children's behaviour is calmer and this may be a reflection of calmer staff, a calmer environment, or the benefit of outdoor play. But whatever the reason we feel that this is a result of the Hygge accreditation.
>
> (Mel Hart, Albion House Nursery)

Our wall of
positivity
Let's be grateful for the good
things we do daily!
Our book of
positivity
Dinosaurs Love
Underpants
Dinosaurs

Journaling

> Fill your paper with the breathings of your heart.
>
> *(William Wordsworth)*

This can be done in a simple notebook daily to reflect on and consider the positive experiences you've had or used as a way of self-discovery and reflection. Taking the time to then read it back every now and again will also help you feel good.

Activity

Take a piece of paper and using the journaling prompts below, have a go at letting your brain flow free of thoughts and record these down.

- When did you last feel awe and curiosity about something?
- The simple things that make me happy are...
- Where would you love to visit and what would you hope to see there?
- What advice would you tell your younger self?

- Re-tell one of your favourite childhood memories
- Which season is your favourite and why?
- What does happiness mean to you?
- What always brings tears to your eyes?
- What have you learnt from children and why?
- What have you done so far this year that you're most proud of?
- Describe the ways nature makes you calm
- Use ten words to describe yourself

Act of kindness

The mirror neurons in the brain copy the response of others. If we do an act of kindness and can see how it makes the recipient feel good then we too receive some of that feel-good energy. We can consider how we may build in a daily act of kindness to our day. Here are some suggestions:

- Write a thank you letter to someone
- Lend a hand to someone that needs it
- Spread by beauty by sending flowers, planting something wonderful or create a homemade craft
- Collect litter in your local area
- Make a cup of tea for a colleague

Movement

Bringing movement into our day is not only important for our physical health but it also supports healthy mental health too. Here are some simple ways you can add more movement into your day:

- Break up intervals of sitting at a computer by standing as you work for 30 minutes
- Take a daily walk over lunch
- Have walking staff meetings with your team
- Take the stairs instead of a lift
- Squat down to the child's level
- While waiting for something do calf raises and stretches
- Walk with a friend in nature

When it comes to bringing more joy into the day my member Laura shares how she combines her own passion for self-care with teaching.

Your journey is yours and yours alone. There's such beauty in starting a course such as the Hygge In The Early Years Accreditation and allowing yourself to fully flow and ebb to every corner of learning, accepting that there is no need to force yourself into a mould but instead, grow.

I try to weave into my teaching practice elements of very light but mindful spiritual practices to positively support the children. These ideas purely came about as I was entering a phase in my own life for self improvement. Not everything that I learn is relevant for the children and I use my own intuitive discernment when considering whether to introduce a new idea. I adore yoga and the benefits of yoga have been celebrated for years. Yoga improves your strength, balance and flexibility, and it is also an aid for beating stress. I decided that I wanted to introduce yoga into my PreSchool timetable each morning as a reset for whatever the children had experienced before they had even arrived at school; to relax their mind and body, to offer them some peace and to set some intentions for our own collective in class. I turn off the lights and play low hang drum music followed by breathing and a short session of no more than 20 minutes. And yes, the children love it!

There are times of the day when I can feel the energy of the group rise, things become a little heightened, behaviour might begin to wobble. So, instead of ploughing ahead with my pre-planned Maths session for example, I'll assess the children and offer some calm with yoga. It's simply a practice of briefly taking some time to calm our body, soul and mind so that we can return to our "work" of learning.

Towards the end of our learning day, we will often sit down with our Speaking Stone and gather in a circle. I have three stones in class at the moment; a rose quartz, an amethyst and a citrine crystal. Each day we will ask a different child to select the crystal that they feel called to and we will then take turns to use the crystal as our Speaking Stone whilst saying "today I am grateful for" I feel that fostering a mindful practice of gratitude each day educates our young children into being aware that it's important to think and thank others in our lives regularly. The most heart warming moments are when the child says, "I am thankful for you!"

(Laura, Learning Lightly)

Activity

Write down everything you've done today and highlight if you've met any of the five pillars of happiness. Make a plan for tomorrow on how you will build each aspect into your day.

If you're able to commit to these daily habits and are consistent with them the benefits will soon start to show.

As well as supporting your own wellbeing and that of your team we can also support the families we work with bring a calmer approach to their home life. You could have a hygge workshop in your outdoor area for parents to join you on, set up a hygge parents noticeboard, like my member Sam Boyd has done, or send home a hygge goody bag for parents when their child starts with you. Inside your goody bag you could include some information on hygge with some top tips for embracing it at home alongside a recipe card, a handwritten note from your child's key person, a teabag, something sweet, a candle to light or a plant to grow at home. Here are some photos of what my member Rachael Relton created for her families.

Chapter four

CORE VALUES

Understanding what you stand for and why it's important will help shape not only your day but the quality of your practice. In this chapter I share an activity that will help you gain clarity on what matters to you and the things that light you up, making sure that you live like a Dane and enjoy every day. This will then feed into the vision you create for your setting or school.

After discovering hygge and taking the time to understand what it means to you the next step is to consider how it links in with what you stand for in life. This can be done by asking "what's important to you?" When we're not sure about this we can find ourselves working in a school or setting that conflicts with our beliefs.

While working as a leader in a school under a headteacher who shared the same ethos for me on child-led learning I was able to teach through my core values. However when the headteacher retired I found myself working for someone who didn't share the same values that I had. They wanted the nursery children to have a one-hour computing lesson each week in the school suite and swapped having time at forest school for an extra phonics lesson. These changes and the daily battle of wanting to do what I felt the children needed added to the anxiety I felt. At times I wanted to leave teaching young children, until one day I realised that it wasn't the career that needed changing. It was the "where" and "how" of how I taught that needed a different plan. This prompted me to find a school that had the same values as myself.

On occasions we can find ourselves in a similar position but we don't always have the confidence to act and make changes. Over time this can then manifest itself into hearing yourself making statements to others like:

- "I've had a rubbish day"
- "You won't believe how I was treated today"
- "I've had enough of working there now"
- "As if I have to stay till 6 pm for that meeting tonight on wellbeing"

DOI: 10.4324/9781003189954-6

- "I'm dreading work tomorrow"
- "I actually can't face being there anymore – I've had enough"

We can then find this going on for weeks, months or even years. During this time it leaves us feeling horrendous, we have declining mental health, putting work first and neglecting family while losing time we will never get back. Instead we have to remember that we're in the driving seat of our own life and it's time to stop complaining, stop thinking that living this way is OK and stop making up excuses for why you can't make a change. We constantly show and tell our children that they can get over hurdles...you don't need to wait for a hand over yours. This is up to you.

The vision for your work in Early Childhood as a school, setting or childminder should also tie into your core values. There should be a core set of beliefs and values that help to guide your everyday practice that support you and the children with an understanding of how your children learn best. It might also be influenced by international approaches and methods that you care about, for example forest school, the Reggio Emilia Approach or Montessori.

If leading a larger group of staff, the vision for your setting needs to include the shared voice of the team. This can be done by giving your staff members some question prompts to complete and then collating these together and looking for common threads of thinking. A collective vision can then be made.

Here are some questions to discover and define your why for embracing hygge in your overall vision.

- Why do you want to embrace hygge?
- Why do you believe hygge is the best way to live?
- What does being calm look like to you in early childhood?
- How can you create hygge in our setting?
- How do young children learn best?
- How would you resource your provision to support hygge?
- What opportunities would the children experience each day?

Here is an example of a vision statement created by one of my members, "A calm, safe environment that benefits the children and me."

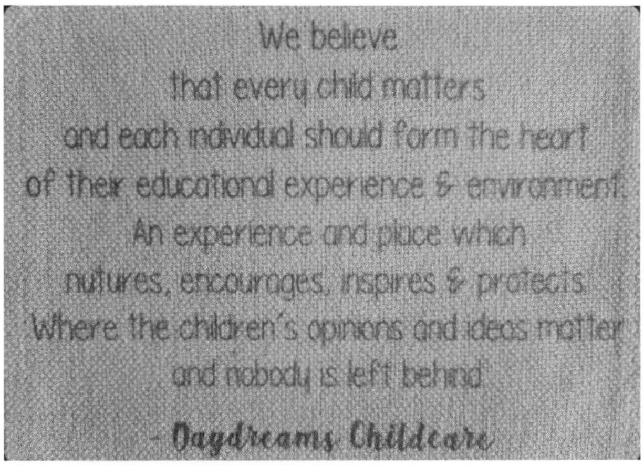

We can think about how we share this with our families, new members of staff and the community. My member Charlotte Fleet from Daydreams Childcare shared her vision by creating a display in her setting. A nursery that I worked with used a video in the entrance to show their vision and how this looked in reality day to day.

The beauty of creating your vision is that it values you as a unique setting. Placing the focus on you not having to be like anyone else. Let your strengths shine and be proud that you're a sustainable setting with composting toilets, or a fully outdoor nursery that embraces nature-based learning in all weathers.

The strengths of each child

The way we see children as learners is an important foundation block when creating the vision for our setting. One of the founding principles of the Reggio Emilia approach is the concept of the "Image of the Child." This "refers to what people believe, understand, and assume about the role of children in education and society."

Here there is a focus on understanding the unique strengths that each child has and taking the time to understand them in order to best understand how young children learn. Our own experiences also greatly impact the way we see children as learners.

> There are hundreds of different images of the child. Each one of you has inside yourself an image of the child that directs you as you begin to relate to a child. This theory within you pushes you to behave in certain ways; it orients you as you talk to the child, listen to the child, observe the child. It is very difficult for you to act contrary to this internal image. For example, if your image is that boys and girls are very different from one another, you will behave differently in your interactions with each of them.

Activity

Take the children in your setting and create a word cloud, or add text over a photo of the child or a self-portrait, of all the strengths you see in the child. Some ideas could be brave, creative, imaginative, competent, wonder, independent and resilient. Your image of the child can then be shared with the child and their families as well as displayed in the setting.

My member Elizabeth Bland created "Wonderful Me" jars as a way of celebrating the uniqueness of each child while also strengthening the relationship with families and setting.

> The children decorated their very own "wonderful me" jars to take home. Their families wrote special notes about what makes their child so wonderful and special to them. It was fantastic because we were able to include many of the people who are special to them, grandparents, aunties and uncles, even their pets! The children brought the jars back in and got very excited to take turns

choosing a special message from their jar and I read them out to everyone. It was such a lovely activity to do and the children were so happy to hear the lovely comments from their parents and extended family members, they beamed as they listened and were so pleased with themselves. We extended the activity by asking them to say what they really liked about each other and I noted it down to add to their jars to keep.

(Elizabeth Bland)

Conflicting values and practice

At times we can realise that the beliefs and values we hold for our setting are not matched up to the everyday practice. For example, I worked with a nursery setting that wanted their children "to become lifelong and independent learners." One look at their early years provision brought up challenges in making this vision a reality. The storage of the resources was not accessible for the children to make independent selections to use in their play. While looking at the planning system in place the children learnt through themed topics with very little opportunity to investigate their own fascinations and curiosities, making the opportunity to become independent and lifelong learners limited.

Another setting wished for their children to "flourish with creativity through play" and when looking at their documentation on the wall I could see that at times children's creativity was diminished by the use of templates with little opportunity to represent the world in a way they desired.

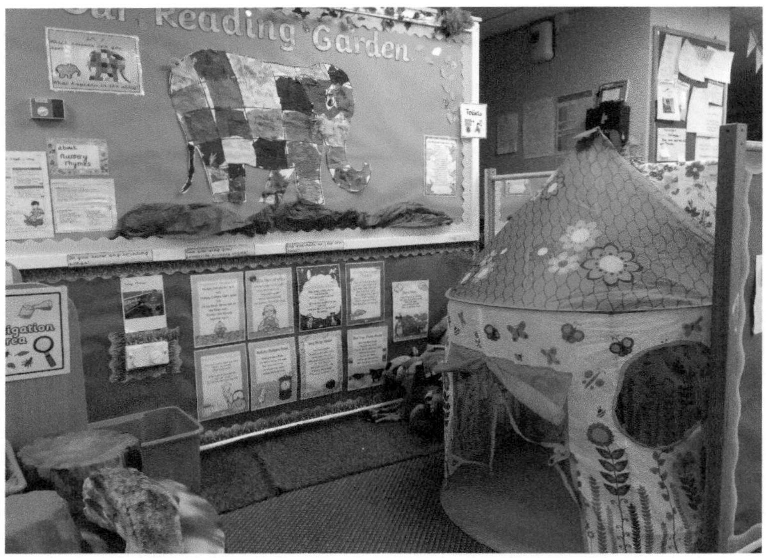

Activity: Matching vision to values

As a team take a tour of your setting (or look at photos of your learning environment) and look at what evidence you can find of your vision matching up. Then repeat by looking at your planning process, daily routine and your policies.

Main takeaways from Part 1

- You can't pour from an empty cup.
- Feeling hygge is unique to all of us and we must take some time to tune into what really lights us up and do more of that.
- Avoid saving the "best" things for the future and bring them into your now.
- Embrace the slower but more efficient pace of life and remember just because you might be doing fewer hours at work now it doesn't mean you're any less dedicated.
- Build time into creating a clear vision in your setting that matches up clearly to your values and beliefs on how young children learn.

PART 2

HYGGE ENVIRONMENT

In a world of Pinterest and Instagram it's easy for us to get inspiration on how to design and set up our provision, but it's important we do the thinking behind why it's been created in a particular way and place our current cohort of children at the centre of the process. The environment is not for last year's group of children or for the senior leadership team to tick a box to say something has been included off a bigger whole school agenda. As I look around the learning space, I like to ask myself "what purpose does this have here?" We want to see how the children respond to the created spaces and develop their classroom accordingly.

The Hygge environment section of the book will allow you to review your learning provision to reduce chaos and bring calm. This section continues to build on your own wellbeing as we look at how we can create environments both at home and in settings that are infused with opportunities for hygge moments while also making sure you have high levels of engagement and that learning is purposeful.

In this section we will focus on:

- Creating a calm sense of arrival in your setting
- Understanding how colour, lighting and layout can impact on behaviour
- Setting up your continuous and everyday provision to have impact
- Resourcing your environment on a budget

DOI: 10.4324/9781003189954-7

Chapter five

A SENSE OF ARRIVAL AND DEPARTURE

Imagine stepping inside your friends' warm cosy home after a long walk in the cold. You begin to thaw out as you notice the lit fire, smell homemade soup coming from the kitchen and your friend greets you with excitement and love. They take your coat and show you to a comfy seat where they offer you a mug of warm tea. In Scandinavia there is a focus on creating spaces where people feel comfortable and welcome. This is called creating a "sense of arrival" and it's the special feeling someone experiences during the first few seconds or so after arriving in your home, setting or environment. This is critical, as it sets a tone and leaves those visiting you reassured and excited while also creating a great first impression. This is how we want your children to feel about coming to work with you each day. We also want the children's family to feel that their children are safe, comfortable and somewhere they will enjoy learning.

One of my favourite times of the year is Autumn and upon arrival at a restaurant while on holiday in Mont Tremblant I saw autumn-leaved foliage weaved onto the fencing as I approached, a beautiful pumpkin patch display and tall lanterns. This made me feel excited about choosing this restaurant to eat at.

Then there was the hair salon I picked in my village when I moved house. There were four different salons I could have gone to but I picked the salon that had a seasonal display in the window, a suspended branch and fairy lights and a smiley member of staff who booked my first appointment. I felt connected to it and could see myself feeling relaxed to have my hair appointment there.

DOI: 10.4324/9781003189954-8

Activity

Consider a place you've visited where you've experienced a sense of arrival and connection upon entry? What elements of the environment gave you these feelings? How did it smell, look, feel?

Remember a place you've been nervous or apprehensive about visiting and brainstorm what about the environment helped you feel at ease and more relaxed? Perhaps it was while visiting a dentist and you were immediately greeted by a warm and welcoming receptionist. The plants and the fish tank also brought a sense of calm to you.

Lastly, reflect on a place you've visited that's not helped you have a great sense of arrival. For me it was my first experience of taking the underground in London. As I walked down the steps to approach the underground firstly the heat hit me, it was so noisy, everyone was in a rush and it didn't smell too great either!

Why does this matter or how does it link to early education? Whether a child is new to you or has had an unsettling morning there will be many different emotions arising as children come into your setting. Especially feeling scared or overwhelmed if it's their very first experience. It's our job to evoke the feelings of ease, excitement and comfort by creating a home from home environment for them. I remember a time when I worked with a nursery and to get to the main entrance visitors passed the bins and to a door where the paint was peeling off. On entering the building, it was cluttered and filled with prams and pieces of old soft play equipment. The first member of staff I met was unsure of the sign-in procedure for new visitors. First impressions are important not only as a selling point for new customers but also to create a feeling of security, calm and comfort for all visiting.

In the Reggio Emilia approach, there is a focus that we should create a sense of belonging in the environment that can connect with the child. This might include a family photo gallery in the entrance, videos playing on a reel of the magical moments of play, documentation that shows a group's child-led interest, an information display for parents and a friendly member of staff that knows the child.

In some Danish kindergartens children and their families are met each morning by the staff with a shake of the hand and a wish of good morning. The shake of the hands is a way of letting parents know that their child will be safe in my hands today.

Activity: What is your sense of arrival?

Leave your setting and walk down the street. Now I want you to approach the entrance to your setting and make a mental note of how it makes you feel. What is the first thing you see? Use these prompts below to help you.

- Does the area look tidy and welcoming around the door?
- Is it safe here?
- Are the signs up to date around the grounds?
- Is it clear where to go?
- Does the doorbell/intercom work?
- Are you greeted by a friendly member of staff?
- Does the member of staff know who you are?
- Does the member of staff give a clear instruction on what you need to do first?
- Is there an area to sit and wait in if you're new here or waiting for a meeting?
- Is it clear in the entranceway how young children learn here and the ethos?
- Do the equipment and environment look clean and well looked after?
- Are the staff warm and nurturing with the children in their care? Especially if one becomes upset and they offer reassurance and acknowledgement of their feelings?
- Is there a cosy little space that children can retreat to if they become overwhelmed?

Here is a list of suggestions on how you could improve your sense of arrival on all the senses:

- Seasonal wreaths on the door.
- Potted plants next to the entrance.
- Lanterns with candles inside on a gloomy winter day.
- Herbs in a bud vase in the entrance can offer a fresh aroma or include indoor plants or flowers (real or artificial) in a vase.
- Homely touches like fairy lights in a jar on a shelf, homemade bunting or lamps on a table.
- Family photos in frames.
- Tidying the entrance hall to make sure it's clutter-free.
- Having a soft mat underfoot with a welcome slogan.

- A display board for parents or information packs available.
- Clean and comfortable furniture that's adult height to sit on.
- Children's key members of staff greeting them on arrival to nursery with a friendly good morning (using the child's name) and a specific comment about the child to create a sense of connection. For example, "Good morning Alesha, I've been really looking forward to seeing you again today. I've popped something in the paint area that I know you're going to enjoy exploring!" and also giving an instruction on when they need to go first. "We're going to be heading to the carpet once you've hung your coat up."
- Staff moving to the child's eye level during the morning greeting helps the child to feel less imitated by a towering adult.
- Is there a special space in the setting that the child can call theirs where they know they can put their belongings and pop any special artwork there that they've done and know that it will be safe?
- Create a transitional space between home and setting where children can pop a special item from home for the day. A shelf with space for a teddy would be ideal.
- Children could transfer into slippers or indoor shoes to add a feeling of comfort.
- Have little displays and objects to promote talk dotted around your entrance way. Some fish in a tank or a nature shelf of interesting finds.

A sense of departure

Just as important as the sense of arrival is for creating calm, the sense of departure is about leaving the child and their families ready and excited to come back again. I have worked in schools where the end of the day can feel manic for everyone involved, with tears at home time for the child that has lost their precious artwork or children that try to leave the designated area as soon as they see their parents walk through the school gates.

Activity

Reflect on your end of day/session routine and how you currently create a sense of departure.

- Do you have systems in place for children to smoothly collect their belongings and get ready for home time?
- Do you reflect on the day you've had and talk about plans for the next time you'll be together?

- Does each child leave you feeling as though they're special and a valued member of the class team?
- Do you have a consistent and safe end of day routine for managing the handover back of children back to family?

A routine I found that worked well was finishing with fantastic learning time where we gathered together as a group and reflected on the day we had. We picked out two children that had shown some key life skills in their learning. For example, "Erin, today I noticed that you were working on a complicated problem in the workshop area. I really like how you took your time and didn't give up even when it was tricky." Then we would sing a song to the two children

> You're a star, You're a star
> What a clever-clogs you are
> You did something wonderful today!
> Well done children, hip, hip hooray!

We would then choose these children to sing the daily goodbye song and name the children that could gather their belongings for home time. Each child could then go to their peg area and collect their artwork from the cubby hole below their peg.

This helped us celebrate the day we had together and finish on a positive that would hopefully inspire future learning to happen. We then opened our gate for families to collect. For larger settings it could be about staggering the position of staff at the end of the session in a way to keep everyone safe. When leading a large Foundation Stage Unit of both Nursery and Reception Children we placed adults at certain positions on the journey out of the school door to the gate, with one member of staff on a closed gate that was opened for each child and parent and closed after them to make sure everyone left safely.

Part of the sense of departure is about creating a link between home and school too. Daily a member of staff would handwrite a summary of the day for parents to read on an easel and include a few photos that had been printed off. Sometimes we would also pop a handout on here linked to the day; a recipe we had tried, a song we had learnt or the storytelling map to a story we loved!

Childminder Vicki Murray likes to finish her day by having a snack together talking about their day before parents arrive.

Chapter six

LIGHTING

For many months of the year the Scandinavians experience 17 hours of darkness a day. If you ever venture into a Scandinavian home, you will notice that although it's very minimalist in design it also feels warm and has a softness to it. Hygge has entered the design world and the cosy atmosphere is created through the careful and thoughtful use of lighting. When we create the correct lighting in our learning environment it can contribute greatly to our wellness and physical and mental health.

Activity

Reflect on your responses to the following questions:

- What are my main light sources?
- Does the room have access to natural light?
- Are there curtains and blinds blocking out the light?
- How many lamps do you have?
- Is there any softer lighting available? (Candles, fairy lights)
- Are areas for reading and focused tasks well lit?

DOI: 10.4324/9781003189954-9

Wiking (2016) suggests that when bringing hygge into your lighting consideration the optimal light temperature is 1800K. This is the same temperature of sunsets or wood burning on a fire and allows you to create a warm glow as opposed to a harshness. This light temperature can also be matched to activities taking place in the early years environment.

Poor lighting is often overlooked in the classroom setting yet it can lead to headaches, tiredness, eye strain, stress and anxiety. Lack of natural light and the use of poor artificial light can contribute to the effects of conditions such as Seasonal Affective Disorder (SAD). Melrose (2015) defines SAD as "Seasonal affective disorder or SAD is a recurrent major depressive disorder with a seasonal pattern usually beginning in fall and continuing into winter months." A study by Dam et al. (1998) surveyed 3556 people in Copenhagen, Denmark about the presence of SAD in their life. Of the respondents,12% indicated the presence of SAD. In the UK it was found that about three people out of 100 experience symptoms associated with SAD.

When creating an inclusive environment, it's crucial that we consider the importance of getting the lighting designed correctly for our children and staffing team. We can consider the use of SAD light panels in our environments. The brightness of the bulbs (needs to have a brightness of at least 2500 lux) in these lights hits the retina and sends a nerve signal to the brain which re-balances the chemicals and hormones which in turn impacts on mood and mental health.

Access to natural lighting is also important as well as how comfortably those in the room can see by using lighting to help with tasks. Consider the reduction of glare, the illumination created and the type of light transmitted. According to a study by the California Energy Commission, classrooms that receive a high level of daylight increase children's progress in maths and English by 20%. The children studying in classrooms with more natural light flooding in also had higher wellbeing scores. Natural lighting can often be achieved simply in our environments by lifting up the blinds and pulling the curtains back.

Harsh overhead lighting can often leave you with a niggling headache due to the flicker of the light as it's transmitted. If it's having this effect on the adult brain imagine how it is making young children feel. It is not only bad for our health but ruins the warm and cosy hygge atmosphere we're trying hard to create. Instead, we can look at creating illuminated pools of light while considering the lighting strategy for each area. The Danes will often create this using candles. In fact, Wiking (2016) reports that half of Danish people light candles at least four days a week. The candlelight creates an energy of movement and it's very relaxing to watch the flicker of the flame. The same effect can be created with wax LEDs on a shelf or in a candle holder on a window sill. You might also decide to add lanterns and candles to

your entranceway through winter to create a warm and homely welcome. My children have enjoyed creating their own candle holders for the setting out of clay, adding holes to the side for the light to cascade and then painting these in white. These have been placed in the centre of the tables at mealtime and the children love watching the dreamy light as it shines beautiful shapes on the table. Glass candle holders on a shelf are also great at amplifying the light and creating a different illumination effect, especially if the glass is etched. As always an appropriate risk assessment should be carried out in setting for the use of candles.

We can also look at using a range of different lighting sources to create areas of contrasting light and dark. This contrast adds a sense of mystery and wonderment. This can be done by placing table lamps, walls lamps and floor lights in strategic places like the dining space or reading area. Or adding a twinkly glow to your window on a winter's day with a Nordic paper star. Through studying on the Hygge in the Early Years Accreditation, Albion House Nursery have made many changes to their lighting plan and now let the natural light flood in as well as having a range of lamps dotted around.

Light and shadow are equally important elements to consider, as they contribute to a feeling of warmth and naturalness.

They also make a very fascinating science concept to explore. My reception children really enjoyed exploring light and shadow in the block area using a projector or in the reading area where there was a space to create a shadow story with puppets. Often the star projector is used on the ceiling during a mindfulness or yoga session with the children and also brings in feelings of relaxation.

Fairy lights help to create a twinkly and magical glow in your learning space and they can be used all year round. These could be placed around a display border, weaved around an indoor plant or added to jam jars on a shelf. My member Jodie Williams often explores adding lighting to her provocations which can add to a new level of intrigue and curiosity.

In my practice I have projected images and videos into my learning environment as a backdrop for learning. When my children were interested in safari play, we projected a live broadcast of the Serengeti safari onto the wall behind the small world play. We've also carried out yoga in front of projected images of sunsets and waterfalls.

As Scandinavian interior design is heavily influenced by nature, we can also combine that with lighting, suspending a branch from the ceiling and covering it in wire fairy lights or adding herbs and fairy lights into a mason jar for a warm glow and placing it on a windowsill.

We can also bring lighting into the way we organise our adult-led activities. There is always so much excitement on a dark winter afternoon to turn the lights off and read a wintery tale by torchlight while drinking warmed milk. My member Sarah Davies has brought light into her daily rhythm with the children.

> Bringing hygge into my setting is one of the best things I have ever done and still enjoy doing. The children love light play, making nature candles, sharing their highs and lows of their day and being outside. When Covid struck last year, it made me evaluate everything and straight away being outside was the way forward for us as setting, not only for our development but for our wellbeing. We became one with nature and seeing the children learning new techniques and recognising flowers, birds and trees was amazing.
>
> As I worked through the hygge accreditation we (me and the children) talked about bringing hygge inside the house more and how we wanted to do this.
>
> We decided on a nature shelf and the children love it and love being involved.
>
> Another thing we now do and enjoy is each day we get cosy after lunch light a scented wax melt (which the children take turns choosing and helping light) and we read a story and one of the daily poems from "I am the seed that grew the tree."
>
> The hygge accreditation has taught me many things but our philosophy is now
>
> "A curious child is a happy child" and the hygge accreditation has not only changed my work life for the better but also my family life.
>
> (Sarah Davies, Sarah's little stars)

In your outdoor area you could explore adding festoon lighting to a loose parts area, stringing outdoor lights along a fence or creating your own ice candles on a snowy day like they do in Finland. Lastly there is something very therapeutic about watching the flames from an outdoor fire dance around under careful supervision and makes a perfect spot for storytelling and campfire treats.

Chapter seven

COLOUR

In this chapter we will dig deeper into aesthetics and the impact colours can have on our mood.

When it comes to interiors many Danes tend to paint most of their walls in white and then pick out a grey along with a softer or warmer accent colour which creates a sense of calm.

Goethe (1810) and his work on the Theory of Colours revolutionised the linking between a colour category and an emotional response. Since then many others (Frank and Gilovich, 1988; Soldat et al., 1997) have also produced scientific evidence to prove this theory. Research on colour psychology shows that the colour choices we make in life are often influenced by our experiences when we were younger, based on gender, age, where in the world we live and our own mindset. Wright (1998) shows that when we get two colours working together in harmony it can have a positive impact on our mental health. Some children may be more sensitive towards colour if they have increased sensory responses (Freed and Parsons, 1997). This may include children with Attention Deficit/Hyperactivity Disorder or Autism Spectrum Disorder. When planning our inclusive learning environment here we must create a careful balance. Clay (2004), Stokes (2003) and Myler et al. (2003) discovered that warm neutral colours help to prevent over-stimulation.

- **White:** The colour white can feel fresh and clean and is associated with peace and tranquillity. White can easily be paired with any other colour.
- **Black:** A powerful colour and often associated with luxury, functionality, black pairs well with red, white and blue for a good contrast. It can be associated with feelings of sadness and depression.
- **Grey:** A neutral colour that is associated with style and elegance. Grey, yellow and pink go well together.
- **Red:** The colour red is a vibrant, bold, attention-getting colour, so preferring this colour might mean you want to project an image of power, action and confidence. Adding this colour to your space is attention-catching and can bring excitement

DOI: 10.4324/9781003189954-10

and passion. Red can also give off feelings of anger and rage and is best paired with white or beige which calm it down.

- **Blue:** This is a calming colour that lowers the heart rate and relaxes. People often describe blue as the colour of stability and safety.
- **Yellow:** According to the experts choosing yellow shows you're a happy person and reminds many of the sunshine. It creates feelings of positivity and optimism and goes well with white.
- **Purple:** The colour purple is linked with feelings of elegance and excitement while lighter shades like lavender calm the senses down.
- **Green:** The colour green evokes feelings of nature and being outside. It creates feelings of harmony, healing and safety.

When babies are first born, they see best in black and white and in our baby provision we should offer opportunities for visual stimulation with the contrast between the bold and light. Perhaps setting up an area of the room that babies can visit that includes different black and white patterns, textures and resources that are frequently changed to sustain interest and curiosity.

When I first started working as a teacher my very first classroom had purple walls, which had been chosen by the headteacher for the calming effects a light purple can have on mood. However, our spaces became a place of over-stimulus due to the way colour was used throughout our environment. Our numerous wall displays were backed in rolls of bright primary coloured backing paper and we had a clashing green speckled carpet with red tables and blue chairs.

Wearing school uniform can have an impact too on emotions (McCarty, 1999) with many children expressing that having it makes them feel safer and at less risk of harm and gives them a sense of belonging to the school community. Yet colour is always important for school leaders to consider when deciding on school uniform colour. Going for a red school uniform can stimulate energy and high emotions while blue can create calm.

Activity

Reflect on the colours in your environment and list how the colours have an impact on emotions.

Chapter eight

SETTING UP YOUR PROVISION

The learning environment is not just about the resources you have in your area. It's about the life skills the children can develop, their attitudes towards learning that are embedded and the way learning is challenged and supported.

In Denmark both the indoor and outdoor learning environments are seen as having equal importance, with the indoors often resembling more of a homely environment that allows young children to develop key life skills in cooking, reading and writing, as well as taking on responsibility for some chores. The kitchen becomes the heart of the setting where home-cooked meals are made daily, little cosy nooks are created throughout the areas to allow young children to snuggle up and read and large cloakrooms provide space to store outdoor clothing and safely store belongings. At Nokken, a kindergarten in Denmark, the outdoor space is referred to as a garden and here there are opportunities to dig deep in the sand and soil, feed the wandering ducks, make dens and work with nature daily. There are no fancy and expensive resources, yet learning happens through the connection the children have to the space and the interactions they make.

Valuing both the indoor and outdoor environment is something Nursery Manager Nikki Moore has worked hard to achieve over the last year.

Being new to early years leadership I had a mountain to climb. I knew in my heart the journey I wanted to take our setting but I lacked the self-belief that I could take the right steps. Every moment of my time at home was focused on work and I was heading for burnout, a place I had been before and was adamant must not happen again. Then, one day, like a metaphorical fairy godmother, Hygge in the Early Years popped up on my social media feed and I knew I had found the guide I needed.

Eighteen months later we spend a daily minimum of 3 hours in our garden or on walks, no matter the weather. Our children are explorers, capable of leading

DOI: 10.4324/9781003189954-11

their learning through play. They are calm, brave, independent and resilient, leaving us ready for their next adventure. Our classroom is an extension of our garden, reflecting the beauty of nature and nurturing the children's budding love for their planet.

By learning to slow down and believe in myself, I have been able to lead my team to realise my vision, whilst rediscovering my love for nature and finding my work-life balance at last.

(Nikki Moore, nursey manager, Graffham Nursery, West Sussex)

We are book-lovers
fum
fi
Jack and the Beanstalk
fi
Jim and the Beanstalk
Raymond Briggs
fee
NORDIC TALES
GENDER SWAPPED
FAIRY

Before starting nursery, school or time with a childminder, young children spend the majority of their time in the home. Many Danish settings create spaces that feel very calm and homely as it brings them comfort by transferring to somewhere with similar surroundings to what's familiar to them. There is extensive research that tells us the impact a positive classroom environment (Dorman et al., 2006) can have on not only the child's learning but also their sense of belonging and wellbeing. When children feel a sense of security and comfort in their learning environment, they are more likely to take challenges with their learning, ask questions and even take risks (Bucholz & Sheffler, 2009) making it vital that we get the classroom learning environment right.

Traditionally in the UK we create an environment to learn in that takes a more formal approach to learning. As a newly qualified teacher I remember inheriting a learning space that was far from homely and calm. There were shelves crammed full of resources, decorations hanging from the ceiling, and so many tables and "areas of provision" crammed into such a space. It was a wonder that there was any room for the 30 children!

My member John and his wife had been childminding for over 20 years and had collected so many resources that they not only forgot what they had but were running out of spaces to store them all. Some of their resources could only be played within one set way like the toy farmhouse and were very rarely used unlike the set of wooden blocks that were used by different children each day to become something wonderful from their imagination or a representation of what they had experienced. After reflection they decided that fewer resources were actually more and this prompted a review of what they had. Having mixed ages also meant that using open-ended materials allowed all children to be creative and challenged in their own individual way. John and his wife consulted the children to ask what they liked and together they began sorting. Some resources no longer needed were given away to children's families while others were passed to charity. When working in this way the children's levels of imaginative play flourished and they had space to store all their favourite resources.

Activity

Audit your resources and consider if they're open-ended. Try taking the malleable area to begin with and using my audit consider how you already resource the opportunities for learning here.

Play dough Resourcing

PATTERN MAKERS	TOOLS
Blocks Combs Wooden Playdough Stampers Q-Tips Textured rolling pins Numicon	Extruders Rolling pins Garlic Press Knives and forks Cookie Cutters Pizza Cutter

LOOSE PARTS		PLATFORMS
Shells Buttons Bottle Tops Pipe Cleaners Googly Eyes Pine Cones Sticks Twigs Glass Gems	Rbbon Feathers Nuts and Bolts Flower Petals Birthday Candles Small world Tea Lights	Tuff tray Bowls Plates Slate Wooden boards Place mats Snack Compartment Trays Cake Boards Mirrors

What do I need to resource now?

When we set up our continuous provision, we are looking to provide a set of everyday resources that are out and available every single day despite who sets this up. For the environment to have maximum impact on the children's learning it needs to be organised and resourced for the cohort of children in the setting now. It's not for last year's group or to tick a box on the senior leadership's agenda for a whole school approach. I like to take a look at my provision and ask myself the questions "what purpose does this have?" and "why is this here for my children?"

Activity

Draw out a plan of your current learning environment and make notes on why you've decided to set the environment up as you have. For example, have you placed the playdough table in a larger space as it's a popular area that your children love to learn in? Or have you removed the specific maths area this year as your children haven't used it and instead there are opportunities to work with maths in every area of provision.

While leading my Foundation Stage Unit in a large primary school there was a requirement that all classes from nursery to year 6 display the same punctuation pyramid poster. As important as it is that children know how to punctuate correctly and have a reminder, it was not relevant for my children and became a piece of wallpaper up on display. Meanwhile it ticked the Literacy Leaders checklist of "teaching Literacy effectively." Instead, we created our own photos in reception of children doing the punctuation actions they had learnt (e.g., air punch for a full stop) and added them to the environment as a meaningful reminder.

When we set up highly successful consistent provision, we are able to provide a set of consistent resources that are out and available every single day despite who sets up. By having the daily repetition here everyone knows what's expected. Imagine if you didn't have consistent provision out. One day Ava almost learns how to ride a bike independently. She is just about getting there with her new skill but the next day when she goes back to try the practitioner hasn't put the bikes out and has the space hoppers instead. How would this make her feel?

When we get our continuous provision right it should:

- Provide everyday learning opportunities
- Allow for repetition
- Encourage independence
- Let children take the lead
- Graft new knowledge onto old
- Consider the age and stage of your children
- Include consistent rules and expectations from all staff on how an area or resource is used

Once consistent provision is in place then you can start to add your enhancements and invitations to deepen learning. My member Emma Thackley has organised her everyday provision in low shelf units that are accessible to the children.

Activity

Draw out a plan of your area and think about the everyday provision and foundations you need. Crawl on your hands and knees and see what the children see. Do they have a sense of "I belong here" when they walk through the door?

If you're working in a home-based setting there is often the pressure to feel as though you're like a nursery and must have all the same areas of provision as one. Instead value your uniqueness. This is something my member Bex Winfield felt:

Before I started the Hygge Accreditation I felt stressed, tired and I always felt the pressure to operate my setting like a nursery or even a school. I used to plan activities based on themes I thought that the children would like and when they weren't responsive to the work and tasks that I set out I would feel deflated and a failure. I was constantly tired and stressed and just felt that I wasn't enough for the children. I wanted to enjoy my work again and I wanted the children to be excited for the activities that we would be doing. After my last inspection where I achieved an overall "adequate" mark I felt that a change needed to be made not only to the setting but for my own wellbeing and the wellbeing of the children attending.

I have now created a vision of that every child matter within the setting by following their interests instead of what I thought they should like. The children know that their voice is important and that their opinion is valued. My setting is more of a "home from home" setting with cosy furnishings and everyday things that will make the children feel that they belong. Parents are all aware of the changes that have been made and feel that their children are better behaved when they go home and are even sleeping better at night.

The main changes that I have made in my personal life is that I no longer feel the pressure to constantly plan what we are going to be doing and I am not up until all hours of the morning printing and laminating worksheet for the children. I make more time for myself and I consider my own and the children's wellbeing above all. We go out daily to the local woodlands whether it's raining or not, we take the time to observe our surroundings and follow the children's curiosity whilst they are outdoors and do not follow a strict timetable. The children love to be outdoors with nature and I find that there is a great improvement in their mood and general attitude when their parents come to pick them up at the end of the day. I have built a shelter in the garden so that the children are able to play outside in all weather. I have made a mud kitchen where children are able to experiment with loose parts and by using the flowers that are in the garden to create a potion etc. Within the playroom I have removed a lot of the plastic toys and have more open-ended resources for the children to play with. The harsh light is no longer used, but rather lamps and fairy lights to create a warm and cosy atmosphere.

I find that I am more calm and happier within myself although on occasions I do suffer with imposter syndrome I just take the time to step back notice the changes that have been made and appreciate how far we have come as a setting. The children are more relaxed, and curious and I also find that they are more willing to try new things and take on new challenges. They have grown to be more independent and are willing to take risks. All of the crafts that we were doing before were very much controlled by myself and they all looked the same. All of the children's work is now unique and displayed on the wall.

(Bex Winfield)

Home-based settings can instead take the home and garden and see it as one flexible space. Consider the key skills you want your children to learn and show where this can happen in your environment. For instance: Opportunities to mark make numbers can happen in the garden through a game of football, using the numicon in the sandpit or as part of your daily routine of counting and writing the number of children in attendance each day. If you're working and living in the same space it's important to be able to clear everything away at the end of the day and switch off. This is important for your mental wellbeing too and needing some downtime. Having sideboard units where resources can be stored away out of sight in baskets helps. A trolley on wheels with mark making resources in or art supplies can also be useful to wheel where is needed.

When it comes to having displays instead of using wall displays you could have moveable displays. For instance, a piece of lattice trellis with string and pegs on to display work. Or flip books to document the learning journey that children can look back at.

As a home-based setting a huge part of your continuous provision is also your physical local area and the opportunities to learn here. Perhaps your local woodland area, library, Post Office and walk to school. These all offer an opportunity for children to learn that should be considered.

For pack-away settings decide what opportunities your children need and create a plan of spaces. Then look at using furniture on wheels, moveable display boards, soft furnishings, baskets, pallets and tyres to zone up your areas. If possible, see if you can negotiate with where you hire the space from for a storage space. This then needs to be super organised with a marked storage box for each area that can easily be taken in and out each session. You could include a photo inside the box so children can help you with sorting what needs to go back in here at the end of each session.

Be creative with your spaces and instead of thinking, "we haven't many tables" consider how you can use different levelled platforms to work off. A cable drum (like my member Sam Herring), a pallet, two tyres with a sheet of wood on top, two wooden chairs pushed together, a wooden crate for a small world scene. For outdoor spaces see if you can involve the children in helping you uncover the sandpit or opening up the shed doors to access

resources. You could also give each member of staff a space to get ready each morning in the 20 minutes or so before you open. At the end of the session plan a group story that might free up some staff members to begin tidying away.

If you're a nursery you may have more space and can consider having more zoned areas for holistic learning to happen. When considering the environment we wish to create for babies and toddlers we want to create a homely and nurturing space where they feel secure.

Consider having the following opportunities for learning:

- **Cubes and platforms** of varying heights that allow little ones to pull themselves up or squat and work at.
- **Construction opportunities and larger loose parts** that allow children to investigate those different schemas we looked at: stacking, lining up and transporting. Have nesting baskets and those with handles available to explore filling and tipping and twisting and turning and natural wooden towers that encourage babies to explore shape and space.
- **Cosy nooks** can be created with wicker archways, low-level wooden partitioning or fencing, clear screens, mirrored cubes or as simple as draping some fabric over the top of a cardboard box. Perhaps get some play tents or a wigwam and invite babies and toddlers to crawl inside and investigate the objects and books there. Add rugs on the floor of your nooks to create areas of softness.
- **Light:** Ideally you would want to be in a space that would let in as much natural light as possible. In my old room the blinds were constantly down and one day I just put them all the way up and what a difference it made! Ahhh sunshine!

  If you're not lucky to have lots of natural light flooding in consider the use of battery-operated fairy lights to create a beautiful twinkly glow. These are great for getting that hygge feeling too and can be displayed around a twig branch you set up, around the edges of display boards or around the frame of a nook. If you use pallets as a platform then insert fairy lights underneath, or add them into jars and vases in your room.

During resting times, you might decide to use the glow of an LED candle placed on a shelf to bring in warmth.

Avoid the harsh overhead lighting seen in many settings and use more lamps.

- **Mirrors** are wonderful for helping young babies and toddlers develop a sense of themselves. Try placing these at a low level in different parts of your room and arrange baskets of resources around these. You could find some Perspex mirror tray inserts to include in your tuff trays so children can explore how things look from a different perspective.
- **Projectors** are really good to use when you have a blank wall or it's painted in neutral colours. Use the projector to create different scenes as a backdrop. For example, projecting images of the sun rising as the children arrive at nursery or a starry sky at sleeping time. I visited a nursery recently that had a video playing of inside a fish tank. There was something very soothing about this.
- **Photographs** are important to have around your setting of the children with their families and taking part in the activities they do with you. Consider sticking these at crawling height like on skirting boards or on the Perspex panels on cots.
- **Sensory play** – and I don't just mean this in the sense of dipping our toes in cornflour gloop! But the everyday opportunities we offer as well by having a range of natural and authentic resources. Having items stored in wicker baskets, wooden bowls and felt sacks really helps to awaken each sense. Think of all those different textures: bumpy, hard, smooth compared to a plastic storage box.
- **A resting place** for an educator to comfort a child is important as these can be distressing times if the child is finding it hard to settle or is feeling under the weather or maybe even share a story. Provide soft and comfortable seating that will support an educator's back. I like to have side tables next to these (like you would do at home) and maybe have a house plant on it or an LED candle in a beautiful holder to try and bring some calm. Include some cushions of different textures and throws to help get comfy.
- **Access to outside** is just so important for this age group but is often not prioritised when setting up provision. In Scandinavia babies spend a proportion of their day outside sleeping and it's shown to improve their immune system. Just get them well snuggled up!

  When they're not asleep give them access to nature.

- **Homely touches:** House plants, photos and prints in frames, clock, little homely touches like wooden hanging hearts or decorate home ornaments. Just think about your living room and create that cosy feeling you get.
- **Baskets with stories, songs, rhymes and puppets** to encourage communication and language skills. Have a range of repetitive board books like *Dear Zoo* that help to build up vocabulary.
- **Wooden chunky small world** with objects that are familiar to young children is good to include alongside your construction. Wooden trains, cars, peg people, farm animals and woodland creatures. I like all of the Grimm's resources.
- **Documentation on the wall:** Create a sense of belonging by sharing artwork, creations and learning on the walls and at child height. When visiting the Sunflower Nursery School in Ontario I liked the way a big white sheet had been used to investigate colour mixing with the whole body.

My member Louise Day, and author of the book *Discover Creativity with Babies* shares how they bring calmness into their provision for babies.

> In setting up provision for our babies and youngest children we ensure that their interests and fascinations are at the heart of what we provide. In order for babies (or any child) to thrive it is important that they not only feel valued and cared for, but that they feel motivated to learn and explore the world by having experiences that will excite and entice them to play. Our environment for babies is calming and mostly neutral with areas for being together and spaces for babies to be alone and rest if they need to. The inspiration for our baby environment comes from the work of Elizabeth Jarman, founder of the Communication Friendly Spaces Approach, our work with the Hygge in the Early Years Accreditation as well as the pioneers of early childhood such as Malaguzzi, Montessori and Steiner.
>
> Creative exploration is a huge part of our ethos at Wallys and is something that we actively encourage the children to become involved with. In order to develop a culture of creativity our resources are accessible to the children at all times and through meaningful observation and interactions, practitioners pick up on cues

from the children about what it is they want to engage with – this intuitive way of working with young children is the most effective way that we can give them early autonomy in matters that concern them and ensure that they learn from a young age that they matter. Our go to activity for young babies or those who are new to the setting is water – its versatility is fantastic for babies as they can explore on their own terms, develop their own ideas (with the support of a mindful practitioner) and use their senses to find out about how it can be used. Babies are sensory learners and as a reflective setting, we are constantly thinking about how we can promote and improve the sensory input our babies receive on a daily. We ensure that we provide opportunities for developing strength in all muscle groups as well as experiences that promote early social skills and language development although, without attentive practitioners who are attuned to the babies they work with, setting up beautiful play spaces becomes meaningless. Our involvement in the Hygge in the Early Years Accreditation really supported our practitioners with this, to ensure that we embedded some of the hygge principles into our own day to day lives in order to slow down and focus on quality observations and interactions with the children rather than observations as a formal box ticking exercise.

(Louise Day, Wallys Day Nursery)

Come on, Daisy

When developing your holistic provision for older children in pre-school or reception consider opportunities for:

- Construction
- Storytelling and writing
- Exploration
- Imaginative play
- Sand and water play
- Painting
- Malleable
- Games and jigsaws
- Woodwork
- Cooking and baking area
- Access to outdoor learning
- Technology

Development of key life skills in the environment and level of challenge

A big part of the Danish culture is building trust and independence with young children and to do this these children are encouraged to take risks. It is not unusual to see four- and five-year-olds climbing trees on their own or using tools at a nature kindergarten in Denmark. Here the culture is on developing the whole child and that means not just focusing on the academic side of learning but the skills needed to be successful throughout life.

We don't have to leave the development of life skills just for the outdoors. We can consider how children develop these skills throughout the learning environment. Many young children in the Danish homes and kindergartens are given household chores to help them learn important life skills and respect their environment. I have found in my practice that children as young as three are very capable of sorting, tidying and cleaning in the provision. Our Friday mornings became "Tidy Friday" where we would take responsibility for the areas we had created by washing, cleaning and re-stocking. This included getting big bowls of water and washing up bubbles, sponges and brushes and cleaning down all of our outdoor kitchen resources, or sweeping the leaves into a big pile for the wildlife, deadheading the flowers in our garden and checking the pens worked and had lids. As a result of doing this I found that the children took better care of the environment day to day. Helping with a chore can also be a useful way to begin building a positive relationship with a child and offer a time to talk one to one.

I remember working with a three-year-old boy with very low self-esteem who had difficulties connecting with those around him and could at times show disruptive behaviour. When reflecting on his background I realised that he was the youngest of five older siblings and at home his behaviour was a callout for attention. In a class of 30 children this was what he was trying to do here too. Having spent some time observing him around others I identified that he liked to feel important and be made to feel special. A way that I was able to work on our child/educator relationship was by saying to him one day, "Lucas, I've noticed how grown-up you are and I wondered if you could give me a hand with an important job." This important job involved washing up our snack cups with me while the rest of the group enjoyed a story. During this precious time Lucas washed the pots and I dried them and put them away. At the end he asked me if he could do that again tomorrow and we made a plan. As the days went by, we used this time to just talk and build up our relationship. Having this time together improved the way Lucas learnt to manage his own feelings and he began to see that I was there as a support not as someone to push away.

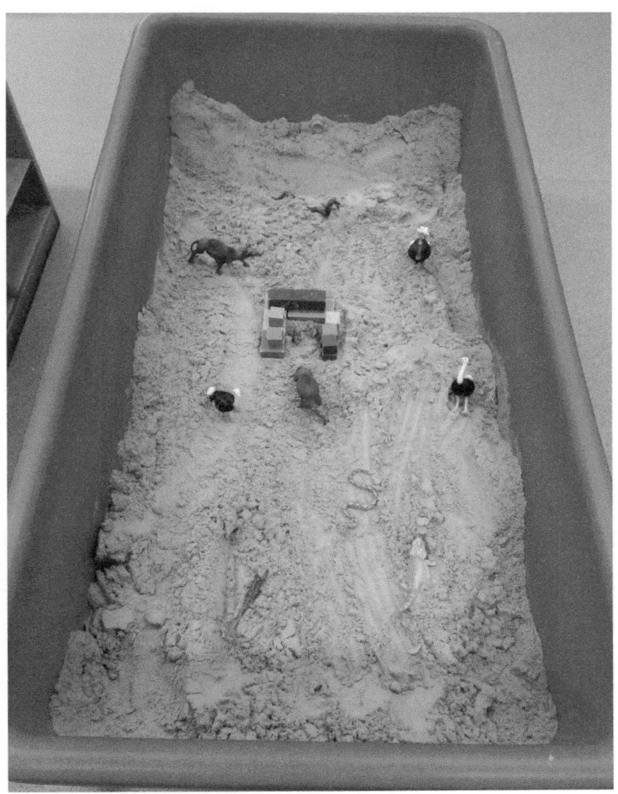

We can also create a level of challenge in our children's skill development. Review your environment regularly and adapt when possible to make sure it fits in with your children's current needs. Create challenge through your use of scaffolding and interactions with the children and teach their next steps through the provision instead of taking children away and to a table. When it comes to having a larger setting or perhaps a school with a nursery and reception classroom you want to ensure that there is progression in the provision on offer. For instance, in my school nursery for two years we had a large sand tray with opportunities for pattern making, digging, pouring and using the buckets and spades. In the nursery provision for three- to four-year-olds there was more of a focus on sand play with the opportunity for language development. Here we added some small-world resources like desert animals, small world people, sand buggies and small blocks to construct with. In the reception classroom there was a deep outdoor sandpit with spades, large trugs and a pulley system that allowed children to develop upper body strength as well as a sand in miniature collection that worked on more precision skills.

We can also involve our children in setting up the environment and having a voice in the environment. Children will respect your environment and use it with higher levels of engagement and involvement if you involve them in the setting up process. Ask your children what they like/don't like about their learning space. When creating a different area try and involve them in the set up. For instance, if they've shown an interest in performing on a stage you might decide to add a stage block to your learning environment. Write a list with the children about what else they might need here. Musical instruments, curtains, costumes, puppets or a microphone? Then start collecting these resources together and involve your children in the process of making the signs as well. The figure shows a reception child designing the backdrop for the theatre role play area.

The way we manage our storage of resources can also help children with selecting and planning their own learning projects. Often, we can have so many resources out in our environment that children can't see or reach what they need. Instead think about your storage solutions. Could you use open storage shelves at child height that not only make it accessible but can be used as a room divider or display? Think clear containers, jam jars, vases, baskets, cutlery tray inserts, wooden crates. My member Claire Wilson created a shed of loose parts outside by displaying all the different collections in clear jars that the children could easily access.

My environment is uncluttered, I have resources at child height for children to access independently. We have soft lighting and fairy lights and I have created cosy spaces for the children. I use lots of loose parts, natural treasures (which we gather on our walks) and vintage, authentic resources which I source from car boot sales and charity shops. Learning is child led not topic led, following my children's interests as well as the seasons and setting up provocations in response.

I love taking learning outside, we regularly go to the woods and parks. I am now developing the ways I bring nature into my indoor environment, adding plants into my invitations and provocations and creating a nature shelf. I look forward to continuing my journey and continuing to bring Hygge into my setting.

(Claire Wilson, childminder)

CLAIRE WILSON
CHILDMINDER
J U N G L E
CLAIRE WILSON
CHILDMINDER

Activity: What do the children need you for?

Stand back in your provision for 15 minutes armed with a pad of sticky notes. Without interacting make a note of every question a child asks you during this time. When the 15 minutes is up take a look and review these. Are you finding that quite a few children need help locating the scissors? Or maybe Eddie didn't know where to put their wet painting. The questions that are asked here can help you change your environment. If no-one knows where the scissors are, get your children together and ask where they should be kept. Invite your children to make their own labels for these. Perhaps it's the sequence of what to do when painting that's a problem. Why not create a photo prompt with the children showing them the order to do things in.

If returning items to the correct place in your environment is becoming troublesome once each area is tidied ask a child to use the camera to take a photo of it. I would then add each photo onto a sheet of A4 paper and pop it onto a clipboard. We would then have a tidying-up inspector each day who would wear a high-visibility jacket and hardhat and who would check each area.

Creating a home from home

At the Hygge conference in 2019 Sally Haughey, Founder of Fairy Dust Teaching, reminded us that each child who enters our setting is meant to be there, that our community is a gift.

For young children we want them to settle and learn here and see it as their space. For the adults we want them to feel comfortable and as though they can be the best version of themselves. Therefore, we can mirror some of the features we may have in our own home that gives us a pleasing feeling.

Activity

Sit down on the middle of the floor in your setting, home, workplace and consider "how do I feel here? What connection do I have here to my home?" Now think about the children you have. Can they see elements in the environment that would be seen also in their own family homes?

Why not add in some:

- Wooden star decorations (we don't have to save these just for Christmas!)
- Foliage and house plants
- Family photos of the children and adults
- Felt garlands (perhaps you'll handmake some)
- Jam jars with flowers from your garden
- Branches suspended from the ceiling with decorations
- LED candles dotted on shelves
- Fish
- Patterned cushions and throws
- Displaying work in photograph frames
- Table lamps and floor lamps
- Decorative pieces

The Danes are big into not only using sustainable materials but also in using the beautiful elements of nature. Science shows us (Schindler et al., 2017) that looking at something stunning makes us feel increased happiness. Why not add that canvas of the beautiful tree you regularly visit to your room, or pop the beautiful sunflower grown in the nursery garden on your window sill? As part of creating a beautiful atmosphere to look at and feel you want to wake up your senses too. How might you use essential oils as part of your daily practice? I used to love spraying lavender in the air before a yoga session or adding lemon into our natural play dough.

Have a look around your setting and make a list of all the beauty of nature you've got. Here is a list of suggestions for you to look out for:

- Stone
- Felt
- Wool
- Wood
- Slate
- Foliage
- Pebbles
- Leather
- Woodland brash (branches, pine cones, acorns)

Toileting

When we consider the element of comfort, we often forget about the importance of creating a space to toilet and change that feels comfortable to a young child. I was reminded about how every detail of the environment is carefully considered and the impact it has on our emotions during a recent trip to Finland.

While visiting Ruka Peak Hotel and Restaurant I was blown away by the amazing floor to ceiling window panel displaying a beautiful view from the toilets of the mountains. The sinks were made out of marble, with fluffy hand towels and beautiful smelling soap. Plants and decorative accessories had also been included in the room and just visiting the space for a short while improved my wellbeing. In what ways can you improve the experience you offer for toileting and changing in your setting to make it a calm place?

In Denmark (Sweden, Finland, Iceland and Russia) over half of the babies and toddlers will sleep and take naps outside in their prams from the age of two weeks old. This doesn't just happen when it's sunny but all year round. Only in temperatures colder than –10 degrees will they be brought inside. Often while walking through the snowy city of Copenhagen, you will see babies snuggled up in their prams outside cafes, with a thermometer tucked in too, keeping an eye on the temperature. Through doing these things babies are building up their immune system and helping them fight off bugs as they get older. At Forskolan Orren, a pre-school outside Stockholm, Sweden, all children sleep outside until they reach the age of three. When temperatures drop colder a blanket is simply added over the pram.

There are now some childcare settings here in the UK that have added sleeping arrangements to their outdoor environment. These include sheltered spaces (and even dream yurts) where babies and toddlers can nap outdoors while supervised by a staff member. All that's needed is a thermal sleeping bag on top of a mattress. Imagine how calming it would be to fall asleep under the trees to the sound of the bird song. Sleeping can also happen for young babies outdoors while in a flatbed pram and they still experience all of the benefits of the great outdoors on their immune systems. When discussing sleep routine, it's always good practice to work together with parents on what they want for their child.

As many of us have over-scheduled time, even the children are rushing from one thing to the next, we want to be creating quiet little nooks and areas of the environment that can be a place to escape when things get a bit too much, daydream or just an area to discover peace in. This could be through a cosy cushioned nook, weighted blanket or sensory lights. It might be a soft chair, plush throw pillow, a beanbag, or even a cardboard box den. You want it to be a place where you or the children can sit and take a breath. It could be a corner, or if you like, an entire room dedicated to relaxing.

Activity

Take a look at your environment and think about how you can offer places that are peaceful. Ask yourself what are the things that make you feel cosy. Is it a warm, handwoven throw blanket? A small table filled with books, pictures and flowers? Perhaps it's being surrounded by an indoor jungle of houseplants. If you have a bit more space, be inventive and it could be a re-claimed rowing boat filled with cushions, an armchair that's been donated, a window seat. If it makes you feel happy and soothed then it will have the same effect on the children. If you're short of space you might have a tent that can collapse at the end of the day, it could be a swing chair in the garden or even some cushions under an upturned table.

I'm also a huge fan of setting up cosy little spaces for the children to engage in small world play. Using an upturned basket, a scene in an apple crate draped in twinkly lights and voile or even some curiosity inside a hat. My member Mel Hart from Albion House Nursery says:

> We feel that the Hygge accreditation has taken us from ordinary to exceptional. The staff look out for each other and go above and beyond my expectations to provide better outcomes for children.

The lunch environment

"How do I bring hygge into the school dining hall?" is a question that I often get asked when working with schools. The honest answer is that you don't! Instead try and make mealtimes a more intimate experience. In Norway and Denmark mealtimes are seen as a time to come together as a unit over some much-loved homemade food. Yet in England meal time feels rushed, noisy and a process rather than an event to celebrate in the day. Not only are young children often fussy eaters but they might be worried about opening their yoghurt, leaving the comfort of a familiar room or being with different staff who support lunchtime cover. When planning lunchtimes these factors need to be considered:

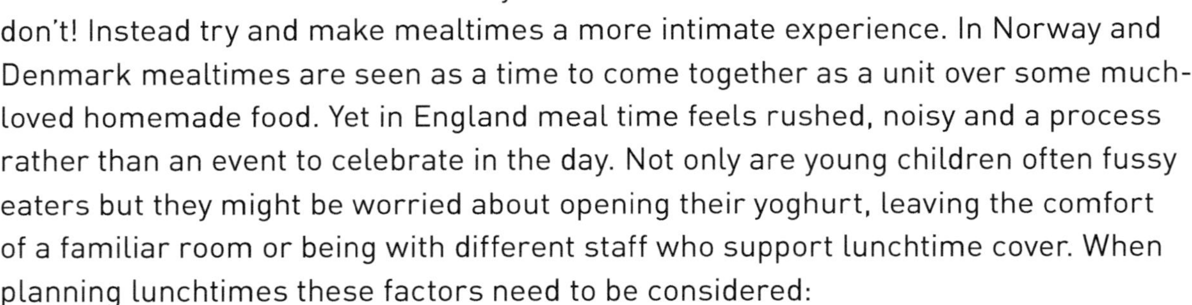

- Are the children in a familiar environment?
- Are the adults familiar to the children and available to support them and talk to them?
- Does the menu offer a variety of choice across the week? Cooked with seasonal produce?
- Is the lunchtime environment calm?
- Do children have a regular seat so they always know where to go? One setting I visited recently had a wooden name tag for each child at lunchtime at the place setting.

- Could children be involved in lunchtime to ease anxiety? Maybe setting the table with a cloth, LED candles, flowers and knives and forks. Maybe they could write the menu, take orders, serve water and have some responsibility. Could you collect some vintage plates to make lunchtime feel more homely?

Is there a way that older children can support the younger ones? Are they able to serve the food or bake the dessert?

If you're a home-based setting where children bring their lunch in pack-up boxes, could this be placed onto plates to make it a more enjoyable experience?

Chapter nine

RESOURCING ON A BUDGET

When we turn our attention to the practice of Reggio, Italy, these schools were built in the hardest hit areas of Italy after the Second World War. With very little money to spend they made sure learning happened through the everyday materials they could find.

Danes will carefully plan their purchases and put thought into the ways they spend. It's not about how much money they make and showing off but actually about how they spend the money to invest in memory making. That's why you won't see lots of new cars driving around Denmark or designer handbags on show. For them experiences mean more as they make you feel alive and bring you together; memories and experiences.

For example, a holiday with the family would cost a lot of money but think of all the wonderful times together and the memories created will last a lifetime. How about buying the seeds for a fruit tree? This is sure to bring returning happiness as the tree grows and an endless supply of fruit can be harvested year on year. One of my great pleasures is to purchase sweet peas in the early spring and enjoy an endless supply of jam jar flowers from them throughout the summer months.

DOI: 10.4324/9781003189954-12

We can apply the same thought process to the way we plan our learning environments. We all perhaps dream of having the Instagram worthy environments we see online yet we are often restricted when it comes to the reality of budgets. In this chapter we look at the Danes' love of the old, antiques as well as upcycling, and the impact it has on the environment, leading to you creating an irresistible environment on a budget.

For those of you working in setting, school or as childminders don't waste your money buying furniture that's made for settings and schools. This is so expensive and all you will end up doing is creating a centre that looks like the one down the road from you. With tight budgets we just have to think more imaginatively.

Instead, we want you to be unique and resource your own by finding it in car boot sales, charity shops, re-cycling and scrap centres or even making it yourself. Having flexible furniture allows for your space to develop year on year based on the children's needs. This is exactly what my member Zoe, a reception teacher, has done.

Finding the perfect items to enhance my Reception setting has been a labour of love and turned into a real passion and perhaps a little bit of an obsession! I scour the second-hand venues and sales, charity shops, local selling pages and car boot sales as well as eBay, Wish, Amazon. Wherever I am I consider how I can use these items to enhance my provision; to bring an element of wonder, to create an aspect of curiosity that goes beyond picking something up for the first time. This intrigue will fuel imagination, invite a friend along for the journey, transform into something completely new or take them to a once uninhabited place. Sometimes it is an unbelievable bargain that cannot be passed up on. I think I have a collector gene from my Romany Nana, whatever it is I feel I just know what works within a setting where the environment is the third teacher.

The authentic items instantly give me a buzz considering the reactions of the children, how they'll play with the item, what knowledge will they bring, how they will discuss and share. I like to place them on the shelves and let them discover the new things during their play. I always explain to parents that it is like going to your grandparent's house and seeing all of the treasures out on view but you mustn't touch them, you mustn't be excitable about them and you can only look on, longingly wanting to put one tiny finger out to test it, touch it, feel its texture and weight; then to understand it more. The difference is that they can explore these treasures at school and they are allowed to pick them up to look closely to see how they work.

I want them to question and to wonder why? They have the chance to use their senses to find their way around these objects. One of my favourite resources I had sourced was 2 old fashioned type-writers. The children could not comprehend that this clunky thing could actually make letter marks on a page. "It's like my mum's laptop but it has no screen!" They spent an extended amount of time feeding in paper, rolling it up and down, whizzing it back to the beginning as they haphazardly hit the keys. It was such a joy to observe. They were extremely proud of their typing capabilities and talked about the "olden days" and began to question how old it was/why didn't they use a computer instead? This opened up so many opportunities for discussion.

I love to look for inspiration from different objects and often find beautiful pieces that radiate everything you'd want from an enabling environment. I never enter my "Aladdin's cave" with a set plan other than in the back of my mind I want authentic, unusual, metal, wood, baskets, loose parts, frames. I search for board games with various player pieces, especially chess or chequers – great for creating patterns, counting, building, decorating; so many options.

When it comes to frames, I remove the glass and the backing, leaving just the frame. These frames are a staple in my setting and can be the starting point in so many ways, encapsulating the children's initial desires and expressing their understanding on using the loose parts available to them. Rolling out old wallpaper across the floor, adding frames loose parts, mark-making tools is another regular activity. It is important to remember that there are always loose parts there to hand, they are familiar and used regularly; and then there are enhancements where different items have been added for a set period of time.

As you walk around my setting you would find various authentic mirrors. I generally go for dressing table types and have now collected quite a few. The mirrors bring a whole new dimension to the play the children are taking part in. They are carefully placed behind the invitation/ enhancement and become part of their learning. They are able to see the reflection, feel the space around them, show emotion and reaction and enjoy watching their creation unfold. I have on many occasions observed children happily talking to the mirror about what they are going to do next. There are so many opportunities for observations during this time as they are often highly engaged. They are taught to be respectful of the items and most of all we trust them to be mindful of the provision and each other.

My most recent find was a solid old, wooden spice rack that rotated with little holes for the pots. This has become the perfect home for our little peg people.

These peg people have no features or clothing, they are plain and can be interpreted in various ways, taking on many roles. I suppose the key to collecting is look beyond what the item is, look for the possibilities and you will only see some of them; the child's imagination will find so many more.

Introducing the environment at the beginning of their time in Reception and reiterating care and compassion, respect and kindness at every opportunity, encouraging discussion and listening to each other; these are just some of the things we do to enable our children to access the environment with this trust and they guide each other to be good role-models within our setting.

New items are added each week, if something breaks, they will be mindful of the delicacy of different materials and they will learn from the experience. Authentic materials are important for the children as they have the opportunity to be part of "real life" and not just a replicate. I have passed on my love and fascination of authentic resources and loose parts to my colleagues and the children; as well as the families. They started their time at school saying "I feel like I'm at home" and "this place is cosy and snuggly!" When we get the environment right, with the right resources true learning will take place with children that feel safe and secure.

(Zoë Clark, reception lead teacher)

Underwood

It's useful to build up collections of loose parts and some of these can be seasonal and offer something unique to the play. In the autumn the woodland floor is a treasure trove of pine cones, acorns, sticks and leaves that are such wonderful learning resources.

Activity

Sit down as a team at the start of each season and consider the loose parts that each season offers.

Here is my list for summertime resources:

- **Natural:**
  - Flower petals
  - Leaves
  - Sticks
  - Seed heads
  - Rocks
  - Flower heads
  - Sliced dried fruit
  - Seeds
  - Beans
  - Tree slices
  - Sand
  - Gravel
  - Water
  - Grasses
  - Sea glass
  - Pebbles
  - Shells
  - Water
  - Bark
  - Tree stumps
  - Seaweed
  - Fossils

Driftwood
Fruit and vegetables
Ferns

- **Man-made:**
  Drain pipes
  Crates
  Buttons
  Grapat wooden pieces
  Eggs
  Plant pots
  String
  Bottle tops
  Glass beads
  Textiles
  Nuts and bolts
  Kitchen roll tubes
  Curtain rings
  Peg people
  Small world
  Drain pipes
  Boat oars
  Car tyres
  Seed trays
  Cardboard box
  Cable reel
  Old picture frames

We can also think about how our areas of provision can be set up using many of these natural or re-claimed resources and the learning possibilities they offer. Here is an example of our outdoor maths shack which was a central hub for resources to be used outside. Children had everyday access to these resources and could use them in any area of outdoor provision:

- Blank wooden number lines
- Wooden number lines with numbers on
- Bamboo sorting trays
- Transparent containers in a variety of sizes
- Blank grids (picnic blankets, google images of grips, garden trellis)
- Weighing scales
- Balance scales
- Wooden numerals
- Natural objects (stones, shells, pine cones, leaves, acorns)
- Number books
- Old photo frames
- A4 and A5 slices of coloured felt
- Fabric ten frames
- Tinker trays (teabag boxes, cutlery insert trays)
- Mark making tools and paper freely accessible to invite children to record their thinking

Another way that I have used natural resources in my teaching is to create an indoor stick centre (that the children also love to add to). It's placed with our block play and offers a variety of different types of sticks (from different trees), different lengths, match sticks, lolly sticks and wooden pegs. One little girl showed high levels of engagement making her own representation of the aeroplane she flew on to Poland. She used sticks and other loose parts to create the farmers' fields (cotton wool balls were also added to represent the snow) that she saw out of the plane window near Leeds and Bradford airport.

Collections of different types of objects also add a level of curiosity and fascination for young children which can be great for developing skills in language development or mathematics. Over a few months I began a collection of spoons that was very popular with my nursery children, who loved to sort them in different ways. We had so many different kinds of spoons: teaspoons, dessert spoons, serving spoons, wooden spoons, slotted spoons, spoons with fancy handles and made of different materials. This then sparked different collections around the interests children had: elephants, hats and socks.

Furniture and layout

When it comes to furniture the Scandinavians are known for their simple and sleek designs, often combining new designs with antique pieces. The furnishings and housewares that emerged from twentieth-century Scandinavia had an enormous impact on modernist design. Due to the abundance of natural materials these remain a key feature of Scandinavian interiors. White pine, ash and beech wood are the preferred types of wood and these can be used for individual pieces, flooring and even the walls. Some of the famous and more well-known Danish designers are Arne Jacobsen, Børge Mogensen and Poul Henningsen and they've really helped to shape interiors around the world.

When it comes to choosing furniture, the Danes often choose a contrast in colour to the normally white or neutral walls. When it comes to choosing the furniture for your classroom and home you can take on a Danish perspective and consider:

1. Choosing something that looks beautiful
2. Is it functional?

Perhaps you could look at creating furniture yourself or sourcing it from a second-hand shop. This also allows you to celebrate your uniqueness and prevent you from looking the same as the nursery up the road. This could be having a set of small nesting tables that can also double as a space to put provocations out on.

Or a stool that can double up as somewhere to sit or perhaps a space to tinker with loose parts.

Within Scandinavia there is a movement in families re-discovering antique furniture and even spending weekends collecting it. There is joy taken in selecting the furniture pieces and becoming fascinated by the memories the pieces must have experienced (like an old dining room table) and also recognising how well the product was made. The past plays a big part in living in such a hygge way and Scandinavians like to acknowledge this. It can be having photos of what the setting used to look like, or old black and white photos of your local area that the children may recognise and enquire about.

Activity

What old or unusual objects could you have in your provision? Working with your team make a list of "wish" type objects you would love to have in your setting. Why not add this to your staffroom and cross it off when anyone finds or donates one. Don't forget to share in your local community as well.

When our environment has been set up successfully with the children in mind, we should see high levels of engagement. This can present itself in a number of ways:

- Children demonstrating curiosity and wonder in their play
- Children having their own interests and fascinations
- Being willing to have a go and try something new as they feel safe and comfortable to take risks
- Problem solving and working things out for themselves
- Being absorbed and concentrating for longer periods of time

Main takeaways from Part 2

- When we take the time to create a wonderful sense of arrival, we can support the emotional and mental health of all children, families and staff spending time in the setting.
- Consideration of how we create pools of illumination can have a great impact on our wellbeing.
- We need to build a learning environment that allows learners to flourish in creativity while also creating our everyday homely yet purposeful provision.
- Explore how children can work with you to have responsibility in carrying out small tasks and in turn develop key life skills.
- Use your environment to celebrate the everyday moments of joy.

PART 3

SLOW TEACHING

In this section we look at the importance of play and how we can slow our planning down by taking a child-initiated approach. This part of the book will show you the exact steps to take to implement it and make it work for you, which, in turn, is going to save you time, improve behaviour and make wonderful learning happen.

Early education in Denmark is not just about focusing on the academic skills needed in life but the skill set young children need to thrive for an unknown future. The Danish curriculum also focuses on how to become good citizens by working on the development of the whole child. In 2009 a survey by the Copenhagen Council explored the values that parents and pedagogues (early educators) feel to be most important for children to learn. These were identified as self-worth, independence, consideration for others and tolerance.

The Danish Early Years curriculum plan (2004) covers the six areas of learning:

- All-round personal development
- Social development
- Language
- Body and movement
- Nature and natural phenomena
- Cultural expression and values

Alongside this early educators must also support the following four learning processes to allow the child to develop as a whole person:

- to be able
- to experience
- to enjoy
- to understand

DOI: 10.4324/9781003189954-13

For Danish children, time in nature forms a large part of their Early Education and there are many "skovbørnehave" (Forest Kindergartens). Evidence from the past 30 years (Barrable and Arvanitis, n.d.) shows that playing outdoors and in nature each day allows the child to effectively meet all areas of the early years curriculum as well as the long-term benefits it has on the child's health.

In the Danish forest schools, "play" is how young children make sense of the world, build relationships, form new connections and really flourish with their learning. Yet why do we often find ourselves moving away from what we know is best with our own practice and turning into a more formal type of approach for young children? I often see in my visits to other schools and settings many young children missing out on learning through play:

- Reception-aged children "learning" through PowerPoint slides that are often re-used each year rather than having first-hand experiences.
- Our special educational needs children who may need extra support getting pulled out of the familiarity of their play and environment for more formal interventions.
- Or how about the child that's found their phonics activity difficult that day? They then have to do extra of the thing they find the hardest and this has to be done taken out of their play later on in the day.
- Then there are the children that are taught about an end outcome rather than the process of learning. This might present itself as identical pieces of the same artwork created by a class of 30 children.

Sometimes the attitudes to learning are that "children can't do certain skills anymore like they used to come into reception doing." If this is the case then it must signpost to us that our way of teaching needs to adapt here too.

Play is important no matter what our age. As adults when we get a new device or a piece of flat-pack furniture that needs building we begin by playing and exploring.

For babies and toddlers play and learning needs is also seen as one. Through whole-body exploration babies begin to learn about their world through the first-hand experiences they have with play. The movement of a wooden toy or the sound of a rattle soon catches their interest and they begin to respond through their different senses and this is how they begin to make sense of the world. Our interactions in the play are also key.

As discussed when exploring the Danish curriculum, play is such an important building block for learning key life skills.

According to a report published by Dell Technologies and authored by the Institute For The Future (IFTF) 85% of the jobs reception children will be doing in the future do not exist today. If this is so, then we need to do everything we can to encourage young children to think outside of the box and develop skills in perseverance, risk taking, critical thinking, creativity and empathy. We want to be encouraging children to discover their own answers and not wait for these to be given. We don't know what tomorrow's world will look like, the COVID pandemic has shown us how much can change so quickly, so we have to provide our children with the preparation to thrive no matter where they live and how they work.

Activity

What jobs are around today that were not around when you were a child? Make a list of these and then take some time observing children at play and consider how in play they learn.

Highlight the statements below that you notice and discuss with your team:

- Using and applying adult-led skills in a range of contexts
- Experiment with risk taking
- Perseverance
- Problem solving
- Togetherness
- Having a deeper level of concentration for longer periods of time
- Gaining confidence and raising their self-esteem
- Being creative
- Higher order thinking skills
- Learning important skills in risk taking, compromise and turn taking

As we move through this section of the book I want to build on the importance of play while showing you how implementing child-led planning is responsive, allows you the freedom to take learning in the direction of the children's interest and develops those key life skills that will allow all your learners to flourish. By implementing these ideas you will also learn how you can re-claim more of your time by reducing your forward planning.

In this section we will focus on:

- Understanding why play is the key building block for early years practice
- Understanding how to go with the child's lead in their learning and ways to document this
- Understanding how to add a level of challenge by setting up provocations to support learning
- Understanding what a high quality interaction looks like and how you can evaluate your own practice to improve the quality of yours

Chapter ten

STARTING WITH AN INTEREST

When I first started teaching I remember around early November time hearing myself say, "This week everything out in provision will be all about Bonfire Night!" I would then brainstorm ideas with my team, often bringing up ideas that had been done for the last few years, and we would search the internet and pinterest for "bonfire night crafts." Once we had a collection of ideas linked to the theme we would then decide on which areas they needed to go in and I would then spend my Planning and Preparation Time school gave me to typing these up into our weekly provision plan. On the Friday night after school I would work hard to laminate resources, collect resources and set up each area ready for the following Monday.

MORNING TIMETABLE **Theme: Funny Bones Wk bg. 02/10/13**

Autumn 1 Rhymes and Numbers		A	Topic focus My Body Funny Bones		
	Monday	Tuesday	Wednesday	Thursday	Friday
	SELF REG / CHOOSING RISK ASSESSMENT Carpet Rules Class signals	SELF REG / CHOOSING RISK ASSESSMENT Carpet Rules Class signals	SELF REG / CHOOSING RISK ASSESSMENT Carpet Rules Class signals	SELF REG / CHOOSING RISK ASSESSMENT Carpet Rules Class signals	SELF REG / CHOOSING RISK ASSESSMENT Carpet Rules Class signals
Input 1 9am	MORNING SONG Registers / Children count Morning Board Visual Time DOTW song	MORNING SONG Registers / Children count Morning Board Visual Time DOTW song	MORNING SONG Registers / Children count Morning Board Visual Time DOTW song	MORNING SONG Registers / Children count Morning Board Visual Time DOTW song	MORNING SONG Registers / Children count Morning Board Visual Time DOTW song
9.05	CI activities and outside Assembly for older chldn	Find Mr S / PHASE 1 PHONICS to 9.15 then CI activities to 9.45	Find Mr S / PHASE 1 PHONICS to 9.20	Phonics Phase 1	Phonics Phase 1
	10am - 10.15 Snack and Milk / singing	9.45-10.30 PE Hall time 1 ****SEE PLAN****** Incorporate beanbag fun	Bake and Create Time Let's make Gingerbread People! Assembly for older chldn@10am	No PE as Hall is required for KS2 children.	10am Retreat Routine of lining up/ taking off shoes and laying still. Nursery Rhyme Peer massage. Circle time on what makes us special.
	10.15-10.40 **SEE PLAN*** Retreat / Circle time	10.30-10.45 Snack and Milk / singing	10.30-10.45 Snack and Milk / singing	Self service snack throughout session. This to be modelled to the children. Focus on name recognition and routine.	Self service snack throughout session. This to be modelled to the children. Focus on name recognition and routine.
	10.40-11.20 CI activities indoor	10.45-11.20 CI activities indoor Welcom? START INTERVENTION ETHAN AND PSED / CLL	10am Assembly / CI play indoor and outdoor START INTERVENTION ETHAN AND PSED / CLL	CI play indoor and outdoor START INTERVENTION ETHAN AND PSED/CLL	CI play indoor and outdoor Bake and Create Time Let's make Gingerbread People! START INTERVENTION ETHAN AND PSED/CLL
Input 11.20	MAT 1 Heads Shoulders Knees and	LIT 2 What happened in Funny bones 3	UTW Simon Says and Heads Shoulders Knees and T	LIT 1 Song	LIT 2 What happened in Funny bones 3

DOI: 10.4324/9781003189954-14

We would see enhancements of themed resources and adult-directed activities like:

- Laminated firework themed playdough mats
- Adding red and yellow cellophane and kitchen roll tubes to the junk modelling table to make rockets
- Putting black sugar paper up on the art easel and luminous paint colours to paint fireworks

Once the children had arrived on a Monday morning we would walk them around the different areas and explain to them how they needed to use the resources there and remind them to find their name and tick it off once they had completed their time in that area for the week.

Twenty minutes into the children's time in provision and we as staff were already feeling as though things were chaotic and could hear ourselves getting broken off as we talked to children who were not "on task." "Stephen have you made your rocket yet" or "We're not building castles this week in the blocks we're making the Houses of Parliament!" Alongside that, we as adults were sat at tables doing the "important" learning with the children we called for. This might have required writing a bonfire night poem or a fireworks maths game. Other moments of the morning involved stopping a group of children from running around the tables inside and helping a few children that looked lost get involved in an activity. By the end of our week we were exhausted from chasing children to carry out their learning in each area of provision and working our way through a conveyor belt of activities.

Now this type of struggle with our practice carried on happening, week after week and at the time we wondered why were the children's attitudes towards learning not always ideal? Why did we get so many interruptions that took us away from getting the important jobs done? How could we improve behaviour? Why didn't some of the children want to complete the activities we had put out for them?

After some reflection we realised that when we had constantly changed the resources available in our environment for the children to use, they not only became unsettled each week due to all the changes but it took away their independence of planning their own learning. We also found that when we decided on the activity to be made in each area of learning it took away the opportunity for children to explore with their own creativity and create representations of how they saw the world. Children were only "doing" what had been set up by an adult in that area. For example, if there is always a challenge for children to make an adult-led craft in the junk modelling space, they stopping thinking for themselves and would never decide to make "a lanyard with their name on it" because they want to play "teachers!"

We also found that when we taught in such a restrictive themed approach there were many times when the themes wouldn't capture the interest of the child which resulted in them switching off from learning. Leading to children showing boredom, poor behaviour or flitting between areas. All leading to poor levels of engagement and interest from the child.

In Scandinavian teaching there is an understanding that taking things slowly is OK and that the adults should be modelling this to the children. This might be a visit to a duck pond and taking time to see all the different types of ducks without the need to rush onto the next thing. Children are also encouraged to learn at their own pace and that they shouldn't rush through childhood or grow up too fast.

While outside at a Danish Forest Kindergarten a group of mixed aged three- to five-year-olds were busy exploring the woodland area. Two girls could be seen constructing a mini den using mosses, twigs and leaves and then creating their wonderfully imaginative stories around fairies. Other children were seen cooking their morning snack on the campfire, under the supervision of a pedagogue while some were taking risks and climbing trees. Learning was happening everywhere!

Moving away from themes

When we move away from themes and topics we are able to create higher levels of engagement with our learners, improve behaviour and also respect each child's individual development journey and interests.

We can begin by making sure we've created a good foundation for our practice which is offering access to a rich continuous learning environment full of open-ended play resources (loose parts, blocks, small world figures and books) each and every day. As discussed in Part 2, the core of the learning environment will stay constant day to day and will be linked to your children's needs.

It will still be important for us as adults to offer inputs that will spark children's interest and expose them to new opportunities and events, however I no longer need to dress each activity around this. In this instance I might lead an input on learning about bonfire night (giving it a hook or a spark for interest) and when children go off into their continuous provision it's up to them if they wish to continue working on this. As they are already familiar with the resources in the provision they can decide if they want to explore how they might make a firework themselves in the paint or be curious about using loose parts (beads, pipe cleaners, match sticks) to represent their experiences of a bonfire in the play dough. It's also OK if a child wants to make an airport in the block area and use the lollypop sticks as a plane to reflect their recent holiday! There, child-led learning is also celebrated.

Here is an example from my practice of how this worked:

> I watched here how you selected the blocks and fences off the shelf to create your own small world scene. "This is the bonfire we went to last night. It was very hot and there was a fence all the way around it so you didn't touch the fire." Sensitive educator interaction and discussions with the child led to the child mark making a sign for her bonfire warning small world characters to be careful!

In between this wonderful child-led learning there will of course be times and opportunities planned in to teach children particular skills based around their development. For instance linking back to our knowledge of the children we might decide they need some opportunity to practice higher-level joining skills in the making area and so we set up an opportunity for this to happen or how about learning how to colour mix with powder paints.

One of my members shared with me earlier that they had been feeling at a loss as to why the children in their reception class had changed so much in terms of their behaviour, recently commenting that it had gone downhill. On reflection she realised that she had slipped back into her traditional practice of over planning adult-initiated enhancements for each area of provision. I encouraged her to take some time to stand back and observe the children's interests and fascinations and use that as a starting point.

> The changes I needed to make were simple with just moving a few key pieces of provision and adding new things based on what I'd heard them say or saw them enjoy doing. I also upped the level of positive praise and the following day I felt I had regained my lovely class again. Children who were squabbling and irritated were back to being calmer, playing for longer and speaking nicer to their friends. Now that I know reflective practice works I need to be more aware of these subtle changes and plan any changes based on what I observe and what they need. Also after observing using the Leuven scales I am now spending more time building connections with those who are lower down the scale and I've already seen a positive change!

Organising your time

The way we organise our day has a big part to play in how successful child-led learning happens. When we limit the amount of time children have to freely play by breaking up this time: planning in assemblies, interventions or group sessions, the children never fully get into the learning flow. Imagine that you're working hard on an important task, it could be report writing, and you have many distractions; your phone flashes up with a notification, a member of your team asks you a question or you get asked to speak to a parent. Breaking off from your work makes it difficult to get back into it. In fact every time we get distracted and broken off from a task it affects our productivity. It can take the brain on average 23 minutes and 15 seconds (Mark et al., 2008) to re-focus again. The same can apply to the children in their learning. They lose their train of thought, the magic in the flow of the learning goes and it might be tricky for them to come back to this again. Therefore we want to limit the amount of activities breaking into the child-led learning time and aim for long blocks of time in the day.

We also want to offer some consistency in the way we organise our week as this can help young children predict what will happen next, helping to create a sense of emotional settlement. I remember a time when my children felt quite unsettled when my weekly nursery timetable looked over-crowded with many interruptions. Every day looked different with assemblies on Monday and Wednesday mornings, forest school on Thursday mornings and computing time in the suite on a Friday afternoon. As every day looked different many young children found it difficult to know what was happening next and this would make some anxious. Where we could we were able to negotiate leaving some aspects out of our timetable by thinking about our children and what was developmentally appropriate for them to attend. For instance instead of taking nursery into the computing suite once a week, where the majority of the time was taken up with logging each of the 30 children onto the computer and practising mouse skills, we added more technology into our learning environment that could be used as part of the provision. Some of these included adding beebots to our construction area, remote control vehicles outside, torches to our dark den that gave the children the chance to use technology for a reason. We then created a consistent weekly routine that was displayed for the children to see using a daily photo timeline of the day indicating now and next.

Consistency is also required with our expectations and rules within our setting in the daily routine. There are times in the day when child learning will need to come to a pause (meal times) and here my team decided that we wouldn't have a big tidy up session before lunch but instead leave the play out. This allowed children that were in the middle of a block model to be able to come back to this during the next session and allowed them to continue with their learning.

Activity

Take a copy of your own weekly timetable and take a look at how much time your children get in the environment without getting broken off to do other tasks or activities. Is there any way you can maximise this time? What activities/group timings are not developmentally appropriate for your children or having little impact on their learning?

It's important to consider the parts of your day where you have fewer calm moments. We found that the transitional times in the day could be the hardest (e.g., moving from continuous provision to tidying up). I found that offering all children a countdown here helped to prepare them for what would happen next. With ten minutes left before we needed to stop and tidy up I verbally let my children know. I would then announce five minutes, two minutes and one minute.

Activity

Working with your team discuss the parts of the day that have the least calmness. Are there patterns to the time of day you or the children find the hardest? What can you change about the routines here to help them run smoother?

When working in a larger team we can organise our team in a way that allows for child-led learning to flow more effectively. This can be achieved by establishing a weekly rota. Depending on the size of your team it would look a little bit like this:

Base boss: Their role is to make sure children are engaged and on task, not wandering around looking lost, following the class expectations supporting children that might need help with toileting.

Adult focus: An adult that may be working on an adult focus task or interacting with children without being interrupted to manage behaviour or toileting issues.

If staffing allows, this way of organising the team can be duplicated in the outdoor environment too and changed on a daily rota where possible.

Starting with a hook

I would like to plan in some adult-led sessions at the start of the session to ensure it didn't break into child-led learning time in the provision. We need to have adult-led sessions to help children have access to new ideas and possibilities as part of their learning process. We must just be careful in getting the balance right and not having too many! I might create a hook linked to the season, an event, a story or interest. I would get my group together and excite them with the hook and then invite the children to carry on exploring this in their own way when entering continuous provision. Some children would carry on this hook and others would head into play with their own agenda. A hook might be showing the children the snails outside and together we might wonder what we already know about these and write this down. We then might think of some new things we would like to learn about snails and these would be recorded on a separate sheet of paper. At the end of our group time some children would happily go off and look for books about snails, build the snails a new home or make food for them. Other children might not be grabbed by this and as I said earlier that's fine and they can go off and explore their ideas. For the children that have continued to explore this we can then record down what they've discovered on a third piece of paper. This not only shows part of our planning process but is also our documentation by showing how we've made the learning process visible. We might capture the process of this learning through photographs, videos and further child voice.

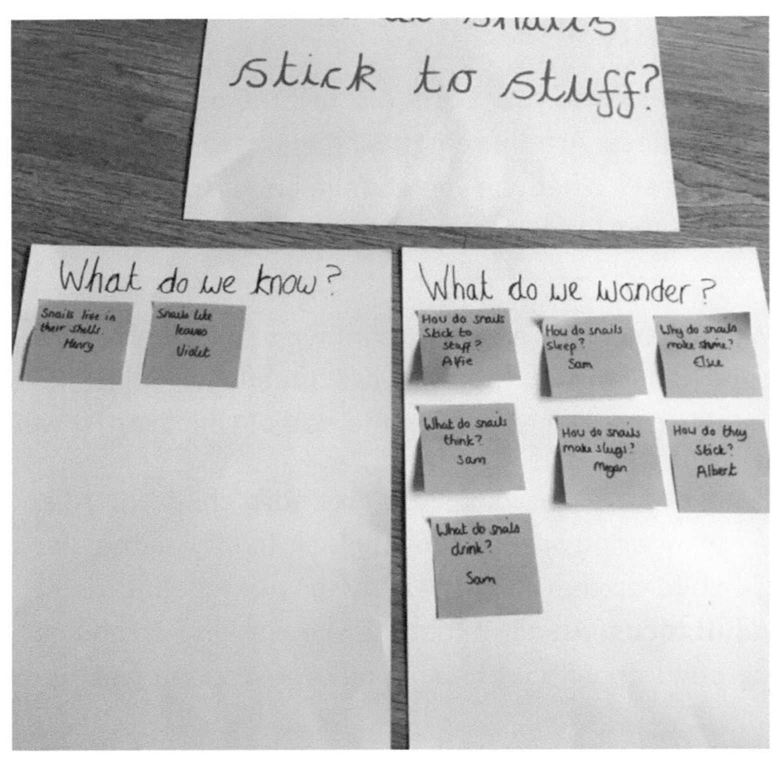

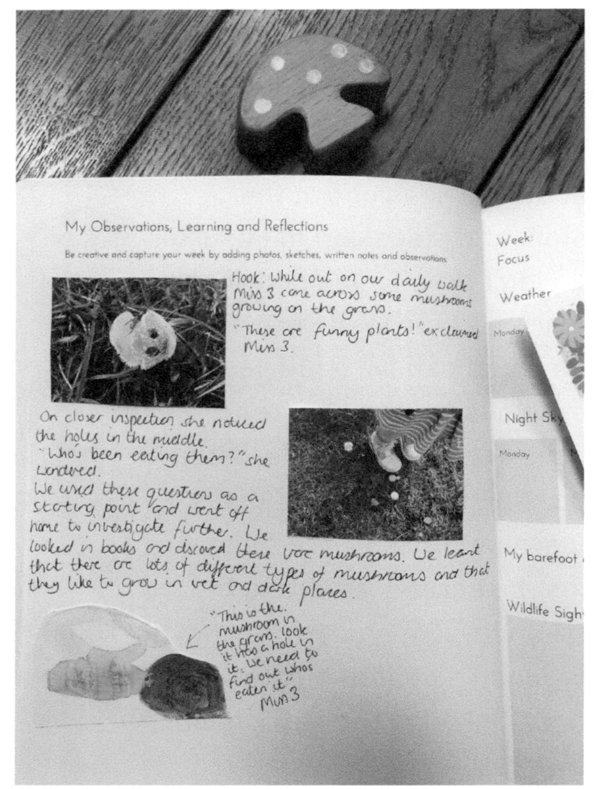

Inspirations nursery use the child's voice and the questions that arise in their learning as a starting point. Recently at Inspirations Nurseries in Horsforth the children were inspired by the moon and embarked on an adventure of Space related creativity and discoveries that began with a home made Rocket.

For many months our Art Studio was over taken with this Space Rocket, we used projectors to emulate galaxies through lights shapes and sounds. We predicted, trialled and tested a range of materials to help us figure out the real material of the moon. We came to our own decisions about our world and Aliens.

During these long projects the Art Studio walls become a canvas, a place to write the child's voice, the windows used to document the continuity of ideas with photos printed. When each long-term project runs its course we transfer their findings onto acrylic boards so their journey of learning is permanent.

When questions are put forward such as "What is After Space?" we can be relieved our role as educators is not to spoon feed children answers but to create an environment for them to test their own theories... and this is one question they're still figuring out.

(from the Art Studio of Inspirations Nurseries, Horsforth)

Child-led learning is the beauty of dropping any prior agenda you as the adult may have and instead letting the voice of the child lead what you do.

Activity: Create a hook

Can you create an adult-led hook that will excite or intrigue your children to learn? Brainstorm some ideas below of what it will involve and the resources you will need.

Lastly consider the pace of your day and ask yourself how often do you allow the children to pause as part of the daily routine? To have a curiosity, a daydream or a question...this is often how learning begins. Do you allow children to walk slowly and wonder about the world around them, offering opportunities to dawdle and see the world for the very first time? We're often so guilty of rushing along and taking children on our own agenda that we forget theirs.

In our rush to get to the next "thing" we have to remind ourselves that it is the process that's important. Not just when it comes to doing an activity but in life in general. While on a walking holiday in Scotland I realised that so many people were rushing to get to the viewpoint on a hike or to reach the top of a fell. I must admit I'm more of a dawdler myself and like to take in the small moments of the hike, the wind through the trees, the smell of the pine or the crunch underfoot. Young children are very good at stopping, looking and being curious as they walk along. Perhaps we can turn to our children to learn this again from them. The importance of slowness and looking at the world through a fresh pair of eyes.

My member Sam Boyd has learnt through the power of reflection to take the time to slow down and let the child lead the learning.

I started a personal journal and at the end of each work day I reflect on the activities of the day and make a note of any new interests coming through, what went well, what didn't go so well – what can be done differently to make it better, and any comments or suggestions from parents. This has meant that the resources available and the invitations to play or provocations that are set up are either aimed at a child's interests or are set up to extend a child's learning.

These changes have meant that the setting is warm and welcoming, that the children are engaged and curious, and nothing is ever dismissed as it is always something we can learn. One thing I set up was our question tree – this was because I realised that when a child asked a question, I would answer it straight away, without any thought of the child and their learning. So, when a child asks a question – such as "Does a dog have an engine?", "How big am I?", "What do foxes eat?" (examples of some of the questions I have been asked recently) – these questions are acknowledged, and we write them down on a label and place them on a tree. This validates the question for the child and allows me time to think how we can investigate the answer. We then find ways to explore what the answer could be – As an example for the child who wanted to know how big they are, we drew around the child, this then was creatively made into a paper version. We used a tape measure to record the exact length, but then also used bricks and other items to measure them. These were placed on the wall and then taken home.

(Sam Boyd)

Chapter eleven

PROVOCATION OR INVITATION TO LEARN?

When we stop dressing each area of provision around a theme, it frees up our time to create enhancements to the environment that are directly linked to the needs and interests of the child, making them have a huge impact on the child's learning.

Here we can set up two or three responsive enhancements to the environment; a provocation or an invitation to learn.

A provocation can come in many different forms, but it is always intended to provoke thoughts, ideas and actions that can help to expand on a thought, idea or an interest. The children lead the discovery and inquiry-based learning here. These are important aspects of child-led learning seen in the Reggio Emilia Approach. By setting up a provocation we are allowing young children to see, experience and make decisions about the world themselves through their own explorations and their interaction with the provocation can involve problem solving, working imaginatively, forming new ideas and making their own conclusions.

In the Reggio approach provocations are set up with open-ended materials with the concept of the child finding their own answers rather than being told them. There is no right or wrong outcome from working with the provocation and the process of the learning is the key. Here the child's unique response to the provocation is celebrated and there is a knowledge that all children see the world individually.

DOI: 10.4324/9781003189954-15

Activity

In the space below I want you to draw your home by following the exact steps I tell you.

1. Begin by drawing a rectangle on a piece of paper.
2. Add a triangle for the roof.
3. Add a chimney on top of the roof on the left-hand side.
4. Draw a rectangle for the front door.
5. Add four square windows to the front of your home.

Now ask yourself, does this reflect the home that you live in? The answer is most likely no. Our homes are all unique and represent those that live there.

As a group of staff now take a look at the sky outside. Using paint create a representation of the sky that you can see today. When you've finished hold these up and compare them with the others in your group.

Even though you have all seen the same sky, the way you process the colours, the shapes of the clouds will all be represented by your individuality. This same concept can be applied to the children too and the way we need to encourage them to see the world in their own way.

Provocations are key for building a strong emotional foundation in your practice and creating a sense of belonging. You're saying to the child – hey I see you, I hear you and I want to be the research assistant with you here so we can discover together.

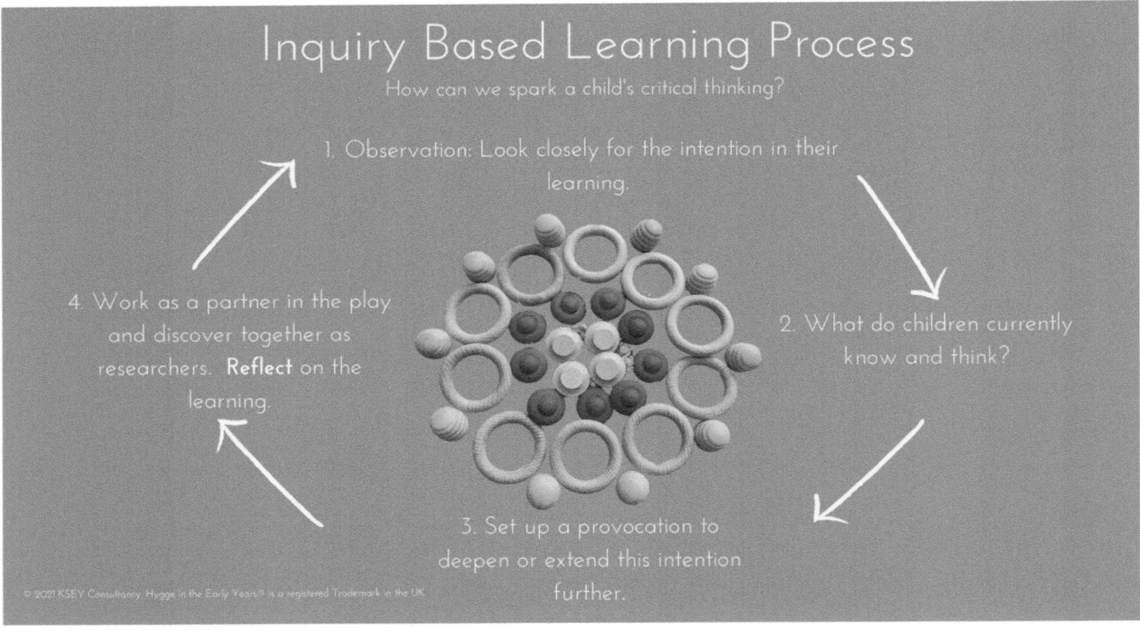

How to set up irresistible provocations

When considering the process of setting up a provocation there is a cycle of process that I developed that makes it easy to follow.

Step 1: Observation to identify an interest, question asked or curiosity. Look closely here for the intention in the children's learning.

Observe the children and find out what makes them curious. This could be the schematic behaviour you see in younger children (e.g. posting items). In older children tune into the questions they ask and interests they have.

Step 2: Understand what the child currently knows around the interest they display through your careful interactions with them.

Step 3: Set up a provocation to deepen or extend this interest further.

Step 4: Work as a partner in their play and discover together as researchers.

Reflect on the learning. Reflect is in bold here as this is the crucial part. If you don't reflect then the work will not have the impact you desire on the children's learning.

Even though you might see a child playing with a Humpty Dumpy toy over and over again you might think that their interest here is in the toy linked to the nursery rhyme. Which could lead you to setting up a provocation on nursery rhymes. But I actually want you to pause and think a little bit deeper. What is actually fascinating the child? Maybe it's the deeper understanding of "why do things break?", "what is the transformation?" or "why does the egg roll?", which could then lead to a provocation around the book *After the Fall* by Dan Santat. Remember to look deeper than the initial interest. Get into the habit of asking yourself what is the big idea here?

When setting up a provocation there are many different materials you can use:

- Natural materials
- Re-claimed and recycled objects
- Silent book
- A visitor
- A collection of objects
- A natural element
- An old object
- A video
- A piece of music
- Light and shadow
- Art material
- A photograph

- Loose parts
- Tinker trays
- Books
- Game board
- Mirrors
- Smells
- Different textures
- Real objects
- Video
- Light

Children can then respond to a provocation you've set up in a number of different ways:

- Music
- Storytelling
- Art
- Sculpture
- Written
- Talk
- Movement

There is often the debate in early education about "should learning spaces be beautiful?" and I believe here it's all about balance and reflection. We can create provocations that pay great attention to detail because we are responding to an emerging interest and we want to captivate the child's awe and wonder even more. We want them to be excited about the possibilities of deepening this learning or fascination so we present it to them in an open-ended and irresistible way.

I also know that amazing learning happens when things are a bit more rustic and even messy, for example, exploring the patterns the numicon plates leave in the shaving foam, the changes to the clay when it's been left outside in the rain or the cardboard box that's been transformed into Elsa's frozen castle with little more than the imagination.

Children and their learning needs can be neglected when we lose sight of what they need. I've seen children experience moments of pure joy and proudness with themselves at mastering a new skill only to be met by an uninterested adult too busy setting up a "beautiful" beach hut role play area that will never be used as intended as it's been created by the adult for an adult theme.

- With everything you always need to consider how does this relate to the needs and interests of the child?
- Is what I'm doing having an impact on the child?
- Who am I creating this for?

I had a small group of children at nature school interested in collecting leaves. This promoted me to take the following actions to set up a provocation for them later on in the day to deepen their learning and interest further.

1. I collected the child's voice, questions and thoughts and recorded these down on paper.
2. I added two books about leaves and trees to deepen knowledge.
3. Some leaf identification sheets were added to support inquiry-based learning.
4. I wanted to include a sensory element so I added rosemary and mint leaves as well as some crunchy leaves to explore.

Sometimes we can create a provocation to challenge a particular way of thinking. I once heard a group of reception-aged children talking around the snack table and one child said, "Children can't look after anything, that's for the grown-ups to do!" The next day I set up an opportunity for children to plant and grow their own flowers from seed, giving them the opportunity to see that children can look after things too and take responsibility.

My member Jodie Williams uses carefully planned provocations in her play to support the individual learning needs.

> Since starting our Hygge in the Early Years Accreditation. We have become a more calmer setting, which I feel is due to bringing more nature based resources into the setting, mood lighting & being outdoors more. Children are engaged more in play & are taking better care of resources. Children love to be outdoors exploring nature & bringing it back to the setting to extend learning. We spend more time playing together in shared play than individual play which has helped the children develop amazing friendships with their peers and helped communication, language & speech for all children.
>
> We now have a lovely collection of natural resources. A variety of baskets containing small logs, log slices, stones, & sticks. Also tinker trays & jars containing smaller natural resources such as acorns, feather, conkers & pebbles. These resources are mainly collected during our daily explorations.
>
> I have replaced most of our one use plastic toys for open ended resources. I have also brought different wooden resources such as wooded numbers, animals & cars.
>
> Bringing nature into the setting has enabled me to set up some fantastic invitations to play & provocations for each child. Natural objects are so versatile in play. I have found that the children are using their imaginations more. We use these natural objects in all areas of the Early Years Foundation Stage.
>
> The children are playing & learning differently to before we brought nature in. Children are able to use their imaginations with just a few objects found on the woodland floor. They can talk about different plants that are growing. They can spot moss, fungi & underground burrows. It's wonderful to see the differences in our setting and children's learning now we are all more in tune with nature.
>
> Parents have noticed that their children are more turned into nature and their surroundings when they are outdoors with family.
>
> (Jodie Williams, childminder)

We can also set up enhancements in our provision to spark a new interest or practice a particular skill. These types of enhancements come from the adult and are a hook that's going to provide children with new interests or sparks a cause and effect. It's important to do these too in our practice as this is how we can inspire new learning to happen.

If we wanted children to practice blend CVC words we might set up an enhancement around something that will grab their interest. If it's a particular season you might have some flowers in a vase displayed on a table along with some loose parts or paint to respond to.

My member Natalie Hull has discovered a real joy in her practice by creating invitations to play.

I offer a home from home childcare setting, I do not have a playroom so I work from my kitchen, living room and garden. So I have limited space and I choose to pack away at the end of each day, so my family and I can relax together and "switch off."

Before I started the accreditation my home/setting had a lot of red colour, I had a lot of laminated labels, harsh lighting, toys only had one purpose and I did not have any plants or nature inside.

Throughout my Hygge journey I slowly changed the environment, I removed the red, and opted for greys and silvers. I removed the labels, and added both real plants and artificial plants. I bought battery operated candles for the children, and real ones for myself, I added fairy lights, and lamps. I have also created a cosy reading nook. It has large cosy cushions for the children to sit on, and I replaced some older books for lovely new ones recommended by Kimberley in both the Accreditation and in the Wanderlust child nature study books. It is so much more cosy and calming here now. I feel more relaxed and calm and I can tell that the children feel the same. This has never been more important due to all the craziness happening in the world right now.

I have discovered a real love for creating "Invitations to play." This is much more enjoyable than writing a plan on paper. Children are drawn to them as they are so beautiful and inviting. I am able to make my best observations of the children when they are engrossed in their play.

I love the quote "There is no such thing as bad weather, only unsuitable clothing." Before I used to say to the children that we will stay inside today as it is bad weather, now though we make sure we go out every day what ever the weather and we always feel so much happier after we do. Nature really reduces stress, and creates so many opportunities for in the moment learning/planning.

We make our own play dough now, and we add natural fragrances, such as lemons on pancake day. We also use real tools rather than plastic toys.

During water play we add natural and real life objects, flowers, vegetables, herbs, and often items the children have picked from the garden, or on our walks:

Maths used to be a planned activity that we completed inside with plastic counters and coloured bowls, now we take our ten frames out with us on walks and visits to the beach (luckily I live a 10 minute walk away from the beach) and do our maths this way.

The Hygge accreditation has created a much better working environment for me, and a more enriched and curious environment for the children. It has given me more quality family time and has taught me about how important my own well being is. What use am I to the children if I am burnt out? I have also learnt to be very grateful for everything I do have, rather than feel upset for the things I don't yet have.

I have completed my accreditation on National Hygge Day 2021, however I feel that my Hygge journey has only just begun as I have so much more I want to do and create for the wonderful children I am blessed with. I feel very excited! Hygge is my way of life now.

(Nathalie Hull)

Planning for interest with larger groups

When working with larger groups or classes of up to 30 children it can become more challenging to see each child's individual interest and respond to this. In Denmark it's common for children to be in family groups of mixed ages. This is often an opportunity to be with siblings and also learn from and support each other.

Working with my reception class I began by placing my children into mixed ability "family groups" that each had a staff member that led them. At the start of every weekday afternoon, we would meet as a family and this would give the children the chance to talk and build up relationships in their group. The adult would act as a scribe and a listener while recording down in the family journal key parts of discussion. Sometimes we would begin by talking about our weekends and our favourite things to do and often other children in the family group would be interested about these experiences and ask more. During this time certain interests would emerge in a group and we would use our time together to explore these further. My group once wondered about where milk came from and other children began to explain their own knowledge to explain it to her. To support this interest further I planned for us to visit a dairy farm one afternoon to explore how some milk gets to us. As the interest was sustained another afternoon we visited our local supermarket and compared all of the different types of milk available; using the labels to learn more about each type. Over a series of days I set up provocations around colour mixing with milk, painting with milk and making our own cheese.

In a different family group one child had explained that their mum's car had stopped working over the weekend. This prompted their next family time session to be outside in the school car park looking under the bonnet of the caretaker's car which then sparked a thread of child-led learning about what makes things go. Open-ended provocations were then set up in the environment to support this interest. A particularly popular one was adding the features of a simple circuit (wires, battery, buzzer, lights) to the junk modelling area to see if children could make their own models go!

Although working in this way will not always provide a particular provocation for each child, through the year it allows the educators to tune into the small group interests that spark curiosity and set up open-ended provocations around this that allow the children to take the lead. Sometimes the interests of another family group might also interest particular children and here there can be flexibility to allow them the opportunity to explore this further.

When setting up provocations we want to try and avoid the following mistakes:

- **Keep it open-ended:** Open-ended play allows the learning to go in the direction the child chooses which allows for not only high levels of engagement and involvement but also creativity too.
- **Stand back and ask/reflect:** Once you've set up a provocation stand back and ask yourself why have I created this? What have I seen/heard from the children that has led to this? Or what opportunities have I identified through my observations that the child needs this?
- **Don't change too quickly:** Often we are in a hurry to change the provision as soon as a particular event is over. For instance taking away all the resources for pancake day as soon as we've celebrated this when actually children need these resources to be left out. This allows them to play with the actual experiences they've had and graft old knowledge onto new.
- **Be responsive:** Traditionally we would have enhanced each area of the provision each week. When planning a provocation we want to be responsive to the

interests/questions asked as quickly as possible to keep the momentum in the learning going. That will mean being as organised as possible with your resources and even having boxes pre-prepared with different areas of interest so that you can get these out when the time is right.

- **Build the provocation around lighting up the senses:** Try and make your provocation wake up each of the senses.

Chapter twelve

HIGH-QUALITY INTERACTIONS

We must recognise that without us as educators learning is not able to be developed and move on without our support. Here there will be the opportunity to explore your own interactions and understand how you can improve these to add challenge and move learning on.

Activity

Consider a recent interaction you've had with a child or one of your colleagues may have had. What aspects of sustained shared thinking do you see? Consider how has this quality of interaction moved learning on? How could you improve the quality of the interaction for next time?

When we take a look at the Danish forest school approach we see that adults are supporting young children outside with taking risks, connecting ideas and challenging themselves in nature. Through their extensive training pedagogues understand when and how to step in and out of children's play. They also understand that their role is crucial and that they can provide time, space and resources which are essential to learning.

I remember the first school I ever taught in while on a teaching placement where only the teaching assistants supported play outside. The staff outside would stand observing the play and interact when behaviour required some support. This offered more of a supervisory approach of "we go down the slide," or "be careful with the sticks" or "put your coat on outside it's cold."

Many years ago I had the opportunity to work on the Effective Preschool Provision Study (EPPE) that tracked the progress and development of children over a time frame of five years and then explored the main components that contributed to a high-quality learning. The Researching Effective Pedagogy in the Early Years (REPEY) project, led by Iram Siraj Blatchford and Professor Kathy Sylva, continued to build

DOI: 10.4324/9781003189954-16

on effective pedagogy. One of the main findings here was around the quality of interactions between staff and child and the impact this could have. You might know of this as sustained shared thinking which can be defined by Iram Siraj Blatchford as,

> the result of two or more individuals (adults and children) working together in an intellectual way to solve a problem, clarify a concept or evaluate activities. It requires all participants to contribute to the thinking and that the thinking must be extended.
>
> *(Siraj-Blatchford et al., REPEY, DfES 2002)*

Iram Siraj-Blatchford describes the elements of sustained shared thinking as:

- **Tuning in:** Listening carefully to what is being said, observing body language and what the child is doing
- **Showing genuine interest:** Giving your whole attention, maintaining eye contact, affirming, smiling, nodding
- **Respecting children's own decisions and choices and inviting children to elaborate:** "I really want to know more about this"
- **Inviting children to elaborate:** "I really want to know more about this"
- **Re-capping:** "So you think that..."
- **Offering your own experience:** "I like to listen to music when I cook supper at home"
- **Clarifying ideas:** "Right Darren, so you think that this stone will melt if I boil it in water?"
- **Suggesting:** "You might like to try doing it this way"
- **Reminding:** "Don't forget that you said that this stone will melt if I boil it"
- **Using encouragement to further thinking:** "You have really thought hard about where to put this door in the palace but where on earth will you put the windows?"
- **Offering an alternative viewpoint:** "Maybe Goldilocks wasn't naughty when she ate the porridge"
- **Speculating:** "Do you think the three bears would have liked Goldilocks to come to live with them as their friend?"
- **Reciprocating:** "Thank goodness that you were wearing wellington boots when you jumped in those puddles Kwame. Look at my feet, they are soaking wet"
- **Asking open questions:** "How did you? Why does this? What happens next? What do you think?"
- **Modelling thinking:** "I have to think hard about what I do this evening. I need to take my dog to the vet's because he has a sore foot, take my library books back to

the library and buy some food for dinner tonight. But I just won't have time to do all of these things"

(Taken from TACTYC Annual Conference Birth to Eight Matters! Seeking Seamlessness – Continuity? Integration? Creativity? 5th November, Cardiff 2005 "Quality Interactions in the Early Years" Professor Iram Siraj-Blatchford)

When we focus on the quality of our relationships we're also tuning into the children and showing them that we genuinely care. This can support the positive attachment we build with the child.

To improve the quality of your interactions you could:

Use video observations: This has to be one of the most powerful lessons you will learn. During my time working on a study looking at sustained shared thinking I had the opportunity to record my audio interactions with children and transcribe them, looking for each component involved in sustained shared thinking. This was such a valuable exercise and I learnt so much about myself from doing this.

As a teacher and a leader, a few of the schools I have worked in used video as a way of reflecting on our practice. It is such a valuable tool and I recommend you try it.

Model interactions outside: As a leader, model what you want your team to practice. This is the best kind of leadership. Talk about why you did what you did and highlight the strategies you've used.

Create prompts: Create key tags that have key question prompts.

My member Sam Goldsworthy uses high-quality interactions as part of her Hygge Friday practice.

Each week the children in our childminding setting are very excited for Hygge Friday, in their own words "Is it Hygge Friday yet?" "It is a celebration."

Firstly we set out some clipboards with photos of two bakes where the children are encouraged to vote for what they would like to bake empowering them to influence the decision. This is done by all the children, the older preschoolers will practise their phonics by writing their name and the younger mindees will purely mark make.

After we have counted the votes and talk about which bake won the vote we gather the ingredients together and bake. Baking regularly gives children the opportunity to learn life long skills and builds their confidence as well as many other rich learning skills such as maths, literacy and turn taking.

In the afternoon we sit down together to enjoy our bakes with a mug of hot chocolate. The children take turns to hand out the bakes and the others will lay the table with the cups and saucers creating a sense of togetherness where we will reflect on our weeks adventures listening to one another.

After we have finished the children will wash and dry their own dishes then place them in the basket for the same again next week feeling a sense of achievement and pride

(Sam Goldsworthy)

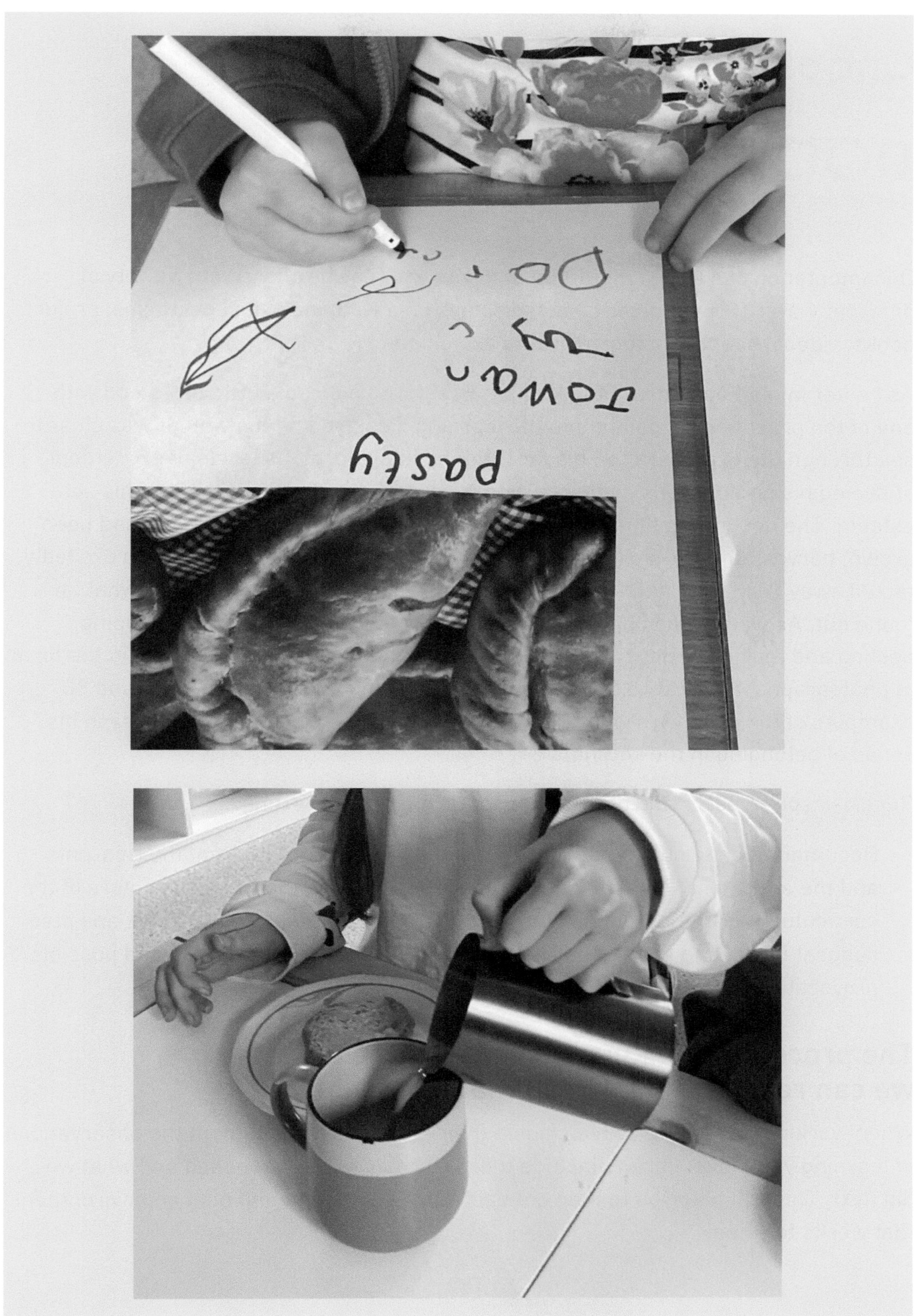
pasty
Jowan

Chapter thirteen

DOCUMENTING LEARNING

Documentation can take a multitude of forms and may be shared in a variety of different ways. Through floor books, displays on a wall, individual portfolios, project books, videos, sound, photographs and exhibitions.

As I enter into a Foundation Stage Unit in Bradford I noticed a little boy stood with one of the practitioners pointing to the learning displayed on the wall. It was clear to see through the expression on his face that he had enormous levels of excitement at seeing his photographs on display and work and in turn this has raised his self-esteem. The documentation was about the exploration of vegetables that had been grown, harvested and then investigated in the nursery garden. As the child excitedly talked away I can hear him looking back on the learning he has done and what he found out. As well as the opportunities he had to learn new skills like chopping, peeling and making soup. The learning that took place had been recorded in the form of photographs, a narrative of the process of learning taken place and 2D and 3D examples of the children's work. Allowing the child to feel valued and increase his sense of belonging in the setting.

Reggio-inspired early educator Marina feels that for her setting

> Documentation should be done with the children for the children, their parents and the educators. With the children because they are the co-constructors of the curriculum, for the parents as they can enhance their learning at home and also suggest ideas, and for the teachers as a medium for self-reflection and possible provocations/invitations.

The process of making learning visible and how we can record the learning that happens

When working one to one with a child in their play you can document the observations of learning you make. I like to include their interest, what's happened and what we did next. This will help you to map out each child's interests and plan an environment that works for them.

DOI: 10.4324/9781003189954-17

This morning I noticed that you were working with such high levels of concentration. You pulled out a building block from the box and each time you did this you looked at it closely, tracing your finger along the edge. You then added it to a tower you were making. You came to tell me that you were building a house. I noticed that your actual fascination was around the way the shapes fitted together. I joined in your play and through this asked you how many blocks were in your tower. You counted them very quickly and said your numbers from zero to nine in the correct order. I modelled 1:1 correspondence when you count. Then I got out the numicon plates and board and gave you the opportunity to see how the plates could fit together while also practising your next step of 1:1 counting.

At Wingate nursery for the past two years it has been my privilege to work at Wingate Nursery School in County Durham. I came to this nursery because I felt that I understood this way of working, I knew (or so I thought) the meaning of "following children's interests" and I believed in trusting children to take reasonable risks. However, it was only through working in Wingate's quite extraordinary (and yet very simple) way that I truly began to understand the meaning and power of these things.

Let me cast my mind back to my earliest days at Wingate and tell you about just a few of the many things that impressed, surprised and downright shocked me! –

- We have only the loosest medium-term plans and no structured "teaching" in phonics, numbers or anything else.
- The children use real tools and equipment (from hammers to step ladders). They are taught how to use them safely and then trusted with them. It's that simple.
- A great deal of time and care is taken with selecting the very best equipment for the children's work – e.g. silk and silk paints, graded colours of powdered paint for mixing, a huge range of wires, strings, cable ties etc – the idea is that every possibility is available so that children are never limited by the environment and their plans can be taken seriously and carried out properly. I remember this having a big impact on me in the early days.
- Independence is at the heart of everything – children independently bake, pull bulky snowsuits on and off, prepare their own snack, serve their own food and much more.

Of all the things that I've learnt at Wingate though, the thing that has had the biggest impact on my own practice has been the power of being deeply reflective. As educators looking for inspiration, we are often given "examples" of what others have done. This can certainly be really useful and it gives us all a "quick fix" of refreshed ideas and set-ups. But what I've learned and loved at Wingate, is how much more effective it is to go back over our own practice and observations at the end of each day to reflect deeply on – "what did I see?", "what do I think was happening here?", "what was my role and how effective was that?", "What (if anything) do I need to do next." The last one, incidentally is crucial, I've learnt that having the courage to do "nothing" is very often the right thing to do.

There is a particular day that sticks in my mind as being quite revolutionary for me in terms of the power of my own reflections. I was working with a group of children to construct a 20ft model of Big Ben (not necessarily something you do every day but this was Wingate after all!). I had absolutely no idea how to build something like this. We'd reached this point by following the children's lead, purely and simply, in such a deep and focussed way as I'd never been brave enough to do before. So, surrounded by huge cardboard boxes (each one bigger than me!) I wondered how on earth I was going to guide these children to attach them together securely. One child in particular saw my worry and after reassuring me that he knew what to do, he climbed the ladders, helped me to cut holes in each box and then trotted off to our studio, bringing back thick garden wire. He threaded and twisted it just the right way to hold those two enormous boxes together. I watched him, I learnt from him, I worked with him. Reflecting later that day, I realised that this little boy had truly taught me about reciprocal and child-led learning. I had no idea how to join those two boxes, but in all honesty why should I have? Why was I naïve enough to assume I was going to "show" these capable children, these designers and architects how to build and attach? They were experts in this. This is what they did every day. I was new to it and I couldn't remember the last time I'd given serious thought to "attaching techniques." So, I happily learnt from them about building and, through my reflections, I realised that they'd learnt from me too – about team work, communication and planning. Together, we created a piece of work that would have been unimaginable to me 6 months earlier. In terms of my own learning, the time I dedicated each day to deep thought and reflection had the biggest impact. I learnt practical strategies that I've used ever since.

When the artist Antony Gormley visited in 2000, he described Wingate Nursery School as "a laboratory of possibilities." We took this to heart and kept it as one of our nursery values, striving each day to maintain this. Working in this unique environment each day and continually reflecting on what we've all learnt is most definitely "the Wingate way."

(Nicola Hesselwood, Wingate Community Nursery School)

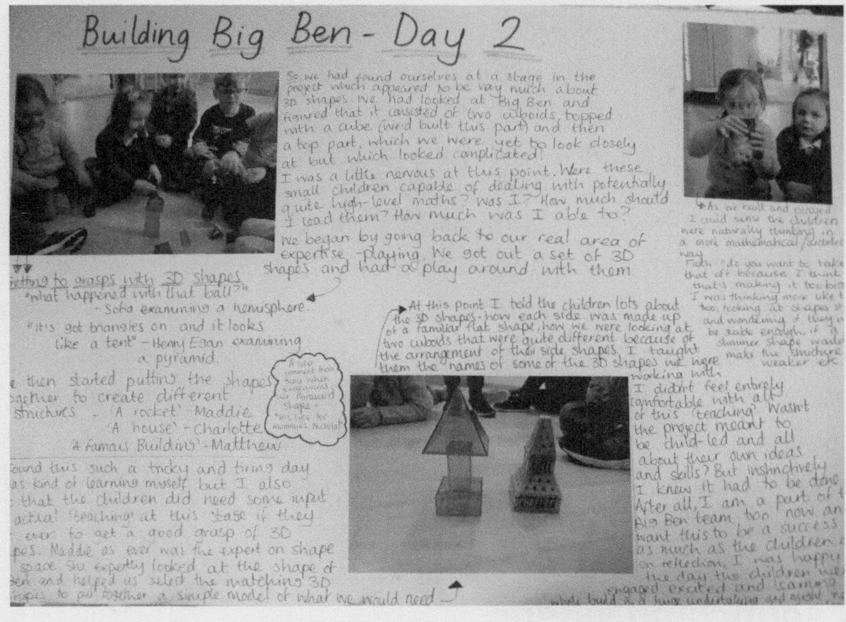

What makes high-quality documentation?

Photographs

Imagine we have a display board with just photographs of a learning experience and a title. Would that contribute to our knowledge of the child? Senior researcher at Harvard's Project Zero (looking at the process of documenting children's learning through creative arts) Mara Krechevsky explains, "Documenting children's learning is an intricate process. Without knowledge of the curriculum and child development understanding it can become a series of pretty pictures without a pedagogical process around it. Understanding theory gives integrity, rigor and meaning to the practice."

Placing an importance on the process of learning, "the basic law of children's creativity is that its value lies not in its results, not in the product of the creation but in the process itself" (Vygotsky). With this in mind it's also useful to think about the way we capture learning in photographs. Do we point the camera lenses at the child with their finished work or are we capturing the thought, skill and emotion that's gone into it? Black and white photographs blown up to A3 size can offer a wonderful insight into the levels of involvement as the child's brow furrows or they stick their tongue out in concentration.

Narrative

As an early educator myself I have always wanted my documentation to be a personal reflection of our time spent together learning, exploring and thinking. As the learning process belongs to the child I have always written up my narrative to them.

As an outsider it is helpful to have some background on the learning that has taken place as this allows a deeper understanding of the process. It can be useful to highlight both child speech and adult interactions to allow others to see how learning has developed and deepened because of elements of sustained shared practice. We can use phrases like, "I modelled," "I asked," "I showed you," "We worked on it together." The narrative can also be a key time to pull together your child development knowledge and understanding of what the child's observed skills, knowledge and schema are.

The use of sound and video

Video and sound allow for the collection of beautiful moments that can be played back time and time again. Perhaps they may be in the form of a video projected onto a blank wall in the setting to allow young children to make connections with their learning. You may also have some laptops dotted around the provision which allows children to watch their learning back and consider new ways of using their skills and knowledge.

Children's creative expression

While working with a setting a few weeks ago I noticed that all the display boards in the baby room were full of photographs. I asked if the setting had a way of showing the creative learning babies were part of. Together we looked at ways babies might be involved in a process like investigating colour mixing with all their body on a large white sheet. This sheet can then be left to dry and then displayed alongside photographs of the process and a narrative to help us understand the learning going on.

As children's creative expression takes a multitude of forms consider ways to display both 2D and 3D artwork of varying sizes. Perhaps you will include shelves in your setting to put creations onto, have clear plastic cases with LED lights to display work in or suspend learning from the ceiling.

Child voice

This offers the most wonderful insight into the thought journey going on; the way children can piece together new knowledge and graft it onto old. Do you record the questions children wonder about and ask? Perhaps these might be the starting point for child-led learning. When working with a group of three-year-olds who had discovered some snails in the soil after a big downpour, there was so much curiosity about what could be seen. We recorded the questions down the children asked on a piece of card titled "I wonder." "Can snails eat worms,?" "how do they move,?" "why do they leave slime behind?" We also labelled another piece of card with "what we already know" and began to collect the children's knowledge on this. Lastly, at the end of our child-led project we recorded a reflective piece on "what we found out."

Parental engagement

We know from a number of recent studies now (study of early education and development (SEED)) that when we offer opportunities for parents to engage and be part of their child's learning then this improves outcomes for young children. Sharing documentation of the children's learning with parents offers them not only an input into their child's learning but allows them to see their child's world.

When do you start to display documentation?

Do you wait till the end and the work is complete? I prefer to start with a blank page or space on a wall and document the process as we go along. This way it scaffolds our thinking and becomes a useful tool.

With every observation of a child consider; does this tell me something that I didn't know before, whether it be in relation to an interest, skill or piece of knowledge. If the answer is no, then it does not need to be recorded.

We must remember that for learning to happen and move forward interaction is key. The work on both Vygotsky's model of the Zone of Proximal Development and the notion of Sustained Shared Thinking helps us to understand the role of the adult as a key component for high-quality learning. We are unable to make this impact on a child's learning if we stand back recording observations with very little interaction and a balance is required.

Alongside this we need to also remember that we should only record the documentation we have time to go back and reflect on with the children. Otherwise what is the purpose in supporting the ongoing learning?

Forest school leader Imogen Ratcliffe feels that embracing hygge allows her to slow down and be in the moment with the children. Even when it comes to the way she plans.

> The Hygge in the Early Years Accreditation has been incredibly affirming. So much of what I already did (candles, snuggly blankets, a daily dose of nature), acknowledged collectively as "Hyggeligt" and its close links with the psychology of happiness celebrated.
>
> The most notable change in my practice as a Forest School Leader has been to ditch any planning and to respond entirely "in the moment." Even the daily timetable has become far more "skeletal" and thus, flexible. Focusing on "being present" and embracing a daily rhythm in nature has meant that we're able to explore every learning opportunity far more organically, without the constraints of planning and restrictive scheduling.
>
> Meaningful provocations include nature and the continuous provision has been stripped back to rich, open ended loose parts giving the children greater freedom in leading their own investigations and telling their own stories.
>
> (Imogen Ratcliffe, Forest School Leader)

daffodils

Main takeaways from Part 3

- When we allow the child's fascinations, questions and curiosities to lead the learning we have improved behaviour, levels of engagement and interest.
- We often move through life at such a fast pace with a fully loaded agenda that we become so busy looking at the "next thing." We must remember to allow the children to be slow, dawdle and daydream. These are important times for connecting the learning together.
- Respecting a child's individual development journey allows the possibilities for learning to be endless.

PART 4

EMBRACE NATURE

The Scandinavian forest school approach has shown us the benefits of taking learning outside all year round and the impact it can have on children's creativity, risk taking as well as child-led learning. Over the last 20 years in the UK the approach to forest school learning has grown and many settings are now developing their practice around outdoor learning. Many early education settings and schools are also spending more time in the outdoor environment as part of their day.

Perhaps this is something you want to embrace more of in your practice but you find yourself coming up against a number of barriers:

- Stuck in a rut and doing the same things over and over again outside finding yourself and the children get bored
- Unsure how to make learning happen outdoors all year round
- Needing support with resourcing high-quality outdoor provision outside
- Lacking knowledge of nature and the outdoors yourself

In this section we take our inspiration from the Danes who embrace not only outdoor learning but also nature as a tool to improve their mental health.

In this section we will focus on:

- The benefits of bringing nature into your day
- How to set up high-quality outdoor provision
- The ways nature can benefit your mental health
- How to embrace the elements of all seasons and find joy
- Ways to bring nature into your indoor environment

DOI: 10.4324/9781003189954-18

Chapter fourteen

BENEFITS OF NATURE

Nature offers us something wonderful and unique that we cannot experience inside. There is a richness and a diversity to what we can experience outside as we go through the flow of the seasonal year and working outside can allow every area of our early years curriculum to be met.

We know from extensive research that being outdoors is good for our wellbeing by raising serotonin levels in the brain, improving mental health as well as allowing children to take risks and build resilience which all contributes to a healthy way of living.

Being in nature and spending our time in this way is part of who humans are. For many thousands of years we walked the land, we lived off the land and our feet were deeply rooted in nature. Over time we've started to spend less time outdoors with technological advances changing the way we live our lives. The work of Sue Palmer (2007) shows us that the increased access to technologies and cultural changes has left the impact of a "toxic childhood," which is causing psychological and physical damage to young children with many adults restricting children's free access to outside over fear of strangers and the risk of injury when exploring, running and climbing. Palmer also explains in her work that the increase in children requiring mind-altering medication to counter depression and behavioural difficulties is also rising in the UK, highlighting the impact of the mental health crisis. The latest data from the UK's Children's Society (2021) shows that one in six children aged 5–16 is likely to have a mental health problem, with many of these children requiring mental health treatment.

Little Lemon Blossom's Childcare show how implementing a nature based curriculum can offer you the opportunity to feel calmer and support mental health.

DOI: 10.4324/9781003189954-19

I started working in the Early Years at a very stressful time of my life with a number of very negative influences around me. I had a clear idea of how I felt I wanted to be working with the children and during my research I stumbled across Hygge, and realised that this was exactly what I was trying to do! I was fascinated by what I was discovering and loved how freely I could incorporate my nature based curriculum within it. As I implemented elements into practice and my everyday life, I was overjoyed to see the really positive reaction that the children had to it. Life and work began to feel less frenetic and I was operating in a more relaxed way, confident now that I had found my path and my instincts had been validated by something tangible! I have been so grateful to the introduction of Hygge into my home and work; Hygge, and actively slowing things down, has made such a difference to my own wellbeing but most importantly, I can see the growth in the children too. We should cherish childhood, curiosity and wonder; Hygge certainly does!

(Little Lemon Blossom's Childcare)

Studies by Velux (2021) show that we are now an indoor generation and without realising it we can spend 90% of our day indoors with lack of light and fresh air. During this time we are often glued to our phones and devices for large proportions of the day. We're even seeing an increase in manufacturers creating products that allow babies and toddlers instant access to technology with devices to fit these onto cots, high chairs and prams, leaving young children's brains addicted to the flashing lights and moving images on the screen and not learning how to play, which in turn is contributing to under-developed muscle development in young children. Think of the grasping, rolling, sitting, standing, running as well as speech, language and communication needs. A lack of tummy time for babies (Trachtenberg et al., 2012) also impacts on the brain architecture of the baby which can lead to developmental delays.

Many young children at Danish outdoor kindergartens are confident at walking and running on uneven ground, climbing trees and balancing across rope bridges due to the rich opportunities they have from an early age. I have recently seen in my practice that some of the young children I work with struggle to work on uneven surfaces of different textures and gradients like a grassy hill or a woodland floor.

Activity

Take a list of the way you've spent your day and attach a time frame to each item to show how long you carried this out for. Then indicate if this activity was spent inside or outside. Now work out the percentage of your time spent outside today.

Laying the roots of the benefits of outdoor education came from the revolutionary work of Fredrick Frobel, in 1837, who opened up his first kindergarten (the children's garden). The aim of his kindergarten was to value the teaching of young children under the age of seven through natural play that allowed young children to blossom and play. His work involved allowing young children the opportunity to work with open-ended materials in a playful way.

When we consider the use of the term "kindergarten" and how it's used today we can see that many of the aspects of fundamental practice have changed since Frobel first coined the term with many kindergartens around the world seeing fewer opportunities for real first-hand experiences and these being replaced with more worksheets, time sat at tables and standardized tests.

> Children are malnourished; eat the wrong things at the wrong intervals. Life for many children is so inert and so unwholesome that they do not digest well. They sit about. They are over clothed. They do not run and shout in the open. They sleep in stuffy air.

Margaret McMillan, a nursery school pioneer, fought strongly in the late 1800s that young children achieved their fullest potential when they had first-hand experiences, fresh air and outdoor play. When we reflect on where we're currently at it's a worry that the situation hasn't changed in the last 100 years for many young children.

In today's world we are battling the effects of climate change and trying to become more sustainable in both our living and our practice. I believe that when we really care about something and think it's precious to us (perhaps it's a treasured photograph of your late grandfather) then we do everything we possibly can to keep it safe. We might put the photograph in a frame away from direct sunlight to help preserve it. The same theory can be applied to our planet. If we can make nature part of everyday life then our children will love it and protect it, making sustainability naturally happen.

With all this in mind, it's time we refresh our approach to outdoor play and consider how we can bring this into our current day practice.

Resourcing for outdoor play

When it comes to babies and toddlers many educators that I work with find it challenging to plan for opportunities for babies and toddlers to work outside in nature.

Below are some ideas for around the year but it's important we don't just save all our outdoor play for the sunny and warmer weather. In Scandinavia babies and toddlers go outside in almost all weather as they believe children need to grow up knowing how to cope with extreme weather conditions. Life can't just stop because of the snow or the ice...otherwise nothing would ever happen!

The important route to making outdoor learning work for all is by wearing the appropriate clothing and footwear. Waterproof suits and layers are always good.

- **Barefoot learning:** Allowing young children barefoot learning opportunities provides a range of benefits from stimulating the senses, developing good posture and foot strength while also developing a connection with nature. Consider how you can plan for opportunities for paddling (whilst supervised) in a shallow stream and provide different textures in your outdoor environment to walk on (grass, sand, bark).
- **Baby carriers:** Getting outside every day with little ones is so important for health and wellbeing. Why not try a baby sling or carrier. Snuggle up together and stay warm – perhaps look at special coats that can be worn over both of you or borrow a larger coat. Go for walks around your local area, the park, a farmers market, the farm, down the canal or even to the zoo.
- **Walks:** Babies and toddlers don't need overcomplicated activities and toys for being in nature. Just being in it with their curiosity at seeing the world for the first time is enough. Just make sure you're an interested adult who can point out the birds or the crunchy leaves underfoot or connect the feelings and words they are experiencing.
- **Picnic blankets and waterproof sheets:** Lay down a blanket or sheet and throw on there some leaves, larger rocks or pinecones to explore. Just be mindful of any choking hazards and don't feel you need to overwhelm them with too much. Holding nature and soil on the hands builds up the immune system as well!

- **Bring nature inside:** Make natural mobiles to hang inside with leaves, flowers and pinecones dangling from a branch as a natural mobile.
- **Have snack time outside:** This is great especially if you're growing vegetables or if you have a fruit tree. You can learn together about where the food the children eats comes from.
- **Water play:** Fill a container up and add leaves and sticks or maybe float flower heads on top or lemons. They will love exploring this with all of their senses. You could even add whisks and slotted spoons to enhance the play. Always make sure you're supervising babies and toddlers around the water activity at all times.
- **Nature treasure baskets:** Create sensory baskets for babies that are full of natural objects.
- **Fallen branches:** Collect some fallen branches and twigs and explore painting these using our fingers or brushes. These can then be dried and displayed in a vase on your nature shelf.
- **The rain:** Put your waterproofs on and go puddle jumping, talking about how the rain feels and the sounds it makes. For non-walking babies take a walk in the pram under a waterproof cover and talk about the rain as you go.

I recently worked in a setting with three- to five-year-olds and together we made changes to the outdoor provision. Here is our story with the reflections and changes we made.

The area currently has many resources that are duplicated from inside like sand and water trays. Some of the areas are quite over stimulating with brightly coloured laminated signs and posters. Asking for instance if the bucket is full? When really this comes from high quality interaction with an adult and children often see these types of signs as wallpaper. The area is mainly concrete and we are working at bringing in more nature. Allowing children to have the opportunities to freely explore and have ideas yet also learn to self-manage risk.

Here are some of the changes we've made:

- Constructing raised beds where children can grow their own plants, fruit and vegetables.
- Zoning off a large beach area for sand play where children can work barefoot and the sand is deep enough to dig deep in and develop upper body strength.
- Created a textured sensory path where children can walk barefoot.
- Logs and wooden planks for balancing on replaced the old climbing frame that was limiting for level of challenge.

- An outdoor seating and eating area
- A space to work with clay outdoors and investigate what happens to it with the rain, ice and sun.
- We have created some weather boxes too. This will let children experience weather through all their senses (e.g., transparent umbrellas to stand under and watch the rain drops.
- Digging patches where children can use real garden equipment.
- Using pallets to create a space to work on natural loose parts.
- Setting up a shed with natural mathematical resources in.
- Zoning off pits of pebbles, gravel, course sand and smooth river rocks for fine motor and imaginative play. Adding construction pipes, scoops and buckets.
- Adding a potted herb garden.
- Adding plants that encourages birds, butterflies and other insects along with some homes for minibeats.
- Planting trees which provide shade.
- Worm farms and compost areas for environmental education.
- Water play areas for sensory play with a dry river bed, boulders, piping, access to a water butt.
- Setting up a woodland kitchen.
- Reading: Books that link to the outdoors may be in themed explorer backpacks with nature detective sheets, compass, maps and notebooks, or a willow reading pod to snuggle up in with a book.
- Construction area: At least 20 crates, wooden blocks, tyres, planks of wood, pulley system, small world, steering wheel, oars for a boat, A3 clipboards.
- Small world on a larger scale using the natural environment as your backdrop.
- Gross motor play: Bikes, wheeled toys promoting co-operation, sand timers for turn taking, PE trolley with a range of equipment, meter stick, dice, timers, cascading bowls and recording equipment.
- Mark making: Painters brushes and water pots, large rolls of paper, sticks in the mud.

My member Jenna has seen a big difference in her practice since introducing books and writing opportunities to her nature provocations.

Through doing the Hygge courses while being at home. I have learnt to use more natural resources in my provocations. Learning and watching the Caterpillars turn into butterflies. Not just putting toys out to be played with. Make it more inviting. Having core books to use for more investigation. For you to support the children's learning.

Adding Maths into the play as well, for counting and sorting. Counting books to do with the provocation like Ten Wriggly Wiggly Caterpillars and Good Night Sweet Butterflies. Props to go with what happens when a caterpillar turns into a butterfly. Having the caterpillars to watch turn into butterflies. Different kinds of butterflies and facts.

Having note pads for literacy and paint to be creative. So they can make notes if they wish.

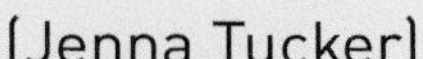

(Jenna Tucker)

Perhaps you live and work in an urban area. Here are some ideas of how you can bring more nature into the space:

- Building raised beds out of sleepers and planting vegetables in them
- Using old pallets as a frame for growing beans
- Growing plants in a length of old drainpipe
- Adding a solar-powered fountain into your tuff tray to explore water
- Adding animal habitats like nesting boxes, minibeast hotels, hedgehog homes and bird feeders
- Dedicate some pots to being cut flower pots where you can grow plants that will be used in play or put into vases

- Have some pots that have bee and butterfly friendly flowers; lavender is always good
- Leave piles of leaves for the hedgehogs and mice to hibernate in over winter
- Add perspex mirrors to look up at the sky and the clouds
- Include a bird bath

You can also use your local area just as the Danes do. Young children take a daily three-mile walk into their local area or to visit a local lake. During this time they become familiar with the community they live in and recognise the seasonal changes.

Activity

Make a list of your favourite places to take the children to experience:

- Grass
- Woodland
- Incline (hills)
- Sunrise
- Sunset
- Water
- Sand

For my members Sarah and Carly their allotment has provided endless learning opportunities for the young children, bringing pure delight at a time of difficulty.

The allotment has been our sanctuary over the pandemic. It's a year today that we had our first visit I can remember it well. What a journey myself and the little people have had we just absolutely love it. We have been blown away with how the children have thrived. The children take so much pleasure in the allotment from cleaning the chickens, collecting eggs, weeding, dead heading flowers, removing male cucumbers, potting on, watering and planting. With a lot of free play in the wildlife garden and woodland kitchen as well. It's a very relaxed vibe down there we love that. The conversations they strike up with other allotment holders and the knowledge they gain from them is just truly amazing. It's an absolute pleasure to be part of. It doesn't feel like work.

(Sarah and Carly Baker Childminding)

Woodland Adventure
hedgie house
2
Welcome
The mud will wash off
But the memories will last
a lifetime

Activity

Working in your outdoor environment take each area of learning and audit the opportunities for learning there. Consider if they bring a level of challenge and support open-ended play. List the resources you could add to enhance learning opportunities.

In 2014 I realised my lifetime ambition in becoming a primary school teacher but I really struggled and received very little support. I suffered crippling anxiety and depression. In 2016 I left teaching and became an independent childminder – the best decision I ever made. During this time I found Hygge. Since studying Hygge in the Early Years I am taking life at a slower pace. I have the freedom to plan around the children's interests; the children love the nature study and are more engaged. I have my weekends and evenings back! We go out on two nature walks a week and through our social media, our community are taking an interest in what we are learning about and what is in our locality! Hygge has changed my life.

(Claire, Flying Start, Keelby)

Chapter fifteen

FRILUFTSLIV

Uncomplicated nature-based play

Nature makes you feel good and the best way to release the endorphins is to get outside each and every day, building in time in nature to your daily rhythm and routine. The Scandinavians are raised to celebrate the seasons from a very early age. It's part of their culture and way of life. In this chapter we explore the Norwegian term of Friluftsliv and how you can bring nature to our day in an uncomplicated way.

Just as the Danish build hygge into their culture, Norwegians have a very special way of improving their wellbeing through the concept of "Friluftsliv" (pronounced free-loofts-liv). This literally means "free-air-life" and is focused on having a simple life that has a strong appreciation for nature. Although this way of living has been part of the culture for hundreds of years it was the well-known playwright Henrik Ibsen who first used the term Friluftsliv in 1859 in his poem "På Viddene" ("On the Heights"). Here the main character in the poem was faced with some troubles in life and in the end chose a free life in nature. We can interpret Iben's use of "Friluftsliv" as "the total appreciation of the experience one has when communing with the natural environment, not for sport or play, but for its value in the development of one's entire spiritual and physical being." Since then the word has become even more deeply ingrained into the way of living in Norway.

I think it's really important to remind ourselves of this and even take inspiration on the way nature can impact the whole self. If we consider how many times we overcomplicate nature, put up barriers to stop us accessing it (with the need of expensive equipment or reluctance due to weather conditions) and the desire to get that "perfect" Instagram shot. When we look at Friluftsliv we can see there is a shift in thinking to it being about getting outdoors in a simple way and just feeling present in the nature around you. Bracken (2020) shares that "In Scandinavia, the freedom to enjoy nature and connect with the outside is as fundamental as breathing, eating and drinking." There should be no need to rush and avoid the temptation to move onto the next agenda.

DOI: 10.4324/9781003189954-20

During my time in Norway there were many days when we would set off for a hike from the house with no particular focus, sightsee or have an end achievement. My Norwegian friends would remind us just to be present without the need for any competitiveness; to have a desire to conquer a mountain or battle raging river rapids in a kayak. Just being was enough. Sitting at the side of a lake and watching out for a moose swimming across or taking a cup of tea on the doorstep and listening to the birds. I'm often reminded of how young children are very good at stopping, looking and being curious as they walk along. Perhaps we can turn to our children to learn this again from them. The importance of slowness and looking at the world through a fresh pair of eyes.

With the harsh weather conditions, especially in northern Scandinavia, the weather cannot dictate the decision to enter outside or not. Instead we can be reminded here of a quote by Alfred Wainwright, "There's no such thing as bad weather only unsuitable clothing." Young children are also brought up with this way of thinking from a very young age. Parents can often be seen walking in the fresh air wearing their young babies in slings all year round. Three-year-olds are taking on daily hikes in the ice and show no fear when it comes to skiing while older children can be seen climbing mountain peaks with their parents with family holidays often experienced in the wilderness. The Scandinavian approach to education also supports Friluftsliv with a strong outdoor approach with many children attending outdoor-based schools working on a curriculum that has a focus on key life skills and understanding the elements of the seasons and natural phenomena. As Jan White discussed at the Hygge in the Early Years Autumn Conference 2020, there needs to be a two-way partnership between yourself and nature. When we learn to appreciate the Earth then the natural love and care for it will happen, which is key to sustainability.

When it comes to learning my member Shelley doesn't feel the need to lead activities with a particular agenda and instead lets the children take the lead.

I signed up to do the Hygge in the Early Years Accreditation during the first lockdown. When the world was slowing down, I thought it was the perfect time for me to slow down too. I completed the Wanderlust Child Nature Study Programme first. I love bringing nature study into our daily routine. We now have a weekly nature table in our provision, which has been a great success. We have something to focus on every week, but in a relaxed and meaningful way. Some weeks, all we do is learn a few facts, read a story or go on a nature hunt and other weeks the children can be completely immersed in a topic. I find having less resources out and more natural and loose parts based materials available, has encouraged so much imaginative and continuous play. I don't plan as many activities, which has given me more time to do the things I love – spend time with my family, go off on little adventures or cuddle up with a good book or movie. The Hygge way of living encourages you to stop and appreciate everything around you, which we have definitely needed this past year. I'm not in a rush to complete my accreditation, I'm just enjoying the slow paced learning journey.

(Shelley Gibson, childminder at Little Lionhearts Childcare)

Robin's
Winter
Song
4
5
robin
Red
robin

Bringing more Friluftsliv into your day:

- Avoid wet playtimes and instead celebrate the rain and the opportunities this gives us.
- Try to avoid overscheduling your day and give yourself time to appreciate and smell the flowers and to see the raindrops balancing on a branch.
- Plan daily time in nature for you and the children where there is no purpose other than to be just there.
- Walk to work or school drop-offs as much as you can and see the same familiar route in different seasons making a conscious effort to notice the changes.
- Introduce walking or outdoor staff meetings with your team.
- Consider how different parts of your daily rhythm can happen in the outdoors; eating, mindfulness, yoga.

Lastly, remember there is no wrong way to do Friluftsliv – just be in nature.

Chapter sixteen

FIND THE JOY IN EACH SEASON

We can be guilty of putting up barriers that stop us accessing nature when we have certain weather conditions like the rain. This chapter is about changing your mindset and seeing the rain as a positive. In doing so it will offer a range of practical ways you can make learning happen all year round outdoors.

While visiting a school recently I overheard a reception teacher panic that the children had brought mud inside the classroom and how the outdoor area needed artificial grass laying instead. "It's rained today and the children have brought mud in with them."

That real connection with nature is so important: the mud, the puddles, the wind. This is how we learn about the world around us and is so important in our sensory development. We can't deny young children these experiences. In fact in my opinion I believe we need to encourage it more. This is when the real magic of early years learning happens!

To overcome the problem of mud inside consider the footwear and clothing the children have to go outdoors in. Perhaps having a welly boot stand? A clothes airer for waterproofs, or a boot wash station? Why not put down a barrier mat in the entrance into the classroom that children can get changed on?

I also believe that for us to teach wonder, curiosity and excitement for the outdoors we as adults need to feel some of this too. When was the last time you felt curious about something in nature? For me it was noticing a blue tit pecking at the outside of the nesting box in my garden. At first I thought he wanted a bigger hole to get in and out of. After researching I learnt that the bird was claiming the nesting box as theirs for the breeding season. Imagine it as putting up a sold sign!

DOI: 10.4324/9781003189954-21

Activity

Write about a time you were last curious outside? How did you address your curiosity?

Use every opportunity to learn

> "Put your coat on Rishi"
> "Jumper on Evie!"

The weather creates a brilliant way for us to learn key life skills but if we find ourselves just telling children what to do they won't always understand the why.

Instead we can use experiences as a learning tool. Sometimes we need to let children go outside for a few minutes without a coat in winter but make sure our adult interactions support a learning opportunity here. Talking to the children about the weather, the way the coldness feels on the skin, wondering with the child what they could do to stay warmer, linking back moments and other experiences: "Remember when we went to the farm last week and the wind was blowing and we were so cold. We wished we had our hats on to keep our ears warm!"

I also like to talk about the weather with the children as part of our morning meeting. Checking the weather forecast together and opening up discussions about what to wear, or to predict what might have happened to our puddles outside.

One of the biggest and positive impacts the training has had is on our outdoor learning. We now have Forest Friday which we started in September 2020. The children spend most of the day outdoors either in their outdoor classroom or in the forest school area. But it's special, the activities we do this day are more than what they would usually access, and the children love it. Every day this week I have had a little girl ask me if it's "wellies today?"

I think I would be in serious trouble if I tried to cancel Forest Friday. This has had a knock-on effect to the other classes in our Foundation Phase department as they are very keen to have their own special outdoor day now.

> Thanks to Hygge, Forest Friday has ticked an amazing number of areas in our curriculum. It is the Foundation Phase philosophy, and it fits in with the Four Purposes of the new curriculum for Wales. We are creating ambitious capable learners, healthy confident individuals, enterprising creative contributors and ethical informed citizens...and it's only just the beginning.
>
> (Joanna Campbell-Griffiths, reception teacher, St Giles School, Wrexham)

Learning for each type of weather

Wind

- Head outside and talk about what senses help us detect the wind. Can we see the wind? Record down the questions the children ask or areas they show curiosity about. Take a walk and look at what shows us evidence of the wind. Think about what we can hear outside. Do the effects of the wind stop when we go inside?
- Explore how we can use the wind for power by showing children photos of windmills. Create your own streamers to use in the wind by tying ribbons onto bamboo rings. Run outside in the wind and explore what happens to your streamer. You could adapt and make a kite!
- Blow bubbles and explore what happens to them and the direction they travel in. Have a go at blow painting by moving blobs of paint on your paper by blowing through a straw.
- Lay on your backs and observe the clouds.
- Make your own wind chimes to hang up outside by using a fallen branch and putting eye hooks into it. Then thread beads, sea glass, shells or metal keys onto your wind chime. Hang it up outside.
- Books to explore together: *Feel the Wind* by Arthur Dorros, *Clouds* by Anne Rockwell, *Rosie's Hat* by Julia Donaldson and *Washing Line* by Jez Alborough.

Rain

- Learn about the amazing work of beavers constructing dams and make a temporary one in a stream.
- Go for a walk outside and look out for rain clouds. Perhaps even take a blanket outside and lay on a field looking up.

- Create a problem that Teddy needs a waterproof den to stay dry in the rain. Explore how you can make this happen outside using a variety of den-making materials. You might want to include a clear plastic sheet and sit underneath it as it rains and watch the drops trickle down.
- Learn about the parts of the world where it hardly ever rains and how some do a rain dance. Can you make up your own weather dance?
- Add rainy day clothing to your dramatic play centre and observe how children use this in their play.
- Create a small world town that's been flooded after too much rain. Talk about the devastation and how the people that live there might feel.
- Go outside and measure the amount of rain we have each day this week and compare it
- Explore re-creating the sound of the rain with rainmakers and other instruments. Sing songs about the rain, such as "Singing in the rain" and "It's raining it's pouring."
- Make boats out of junk modelling and see if they will float in a puddle
- Books to explore together: *Rhythm of Rain* by Grahame Baker-Smith, *Once Upon a Raindrop: The Story of Water* by James Carter, *The Rain Stomper* by Addie Boswell, *A River* by Marc Martin and *Lila and the Secret of Rain* by David Conway.

Sunshine

- Go outside on a sunny day and talk about what you can see. What are shadows? How are these made? Can we create our own shadows? Do shadows change? Record down the children's curiosities as a starting point. You might decide to draw around the shadows in chalk and see how these change throughout the day. You might explore shadows under a tree or the shadows of objects with holes in them (slotted spoons, cheese grater).
- Explore shadows inside by adding torches and lamps to block play and see if shadows can be made of the models. Investigate how we can use shadows to tell stories. Create and set up your own shadow puppet show!
- Take a look at reflection by placing coloured magnatiles, cellophane or coloured blocks in the window and watching their colours reflect. Can we mix colours together? What do we predict will happen?
- Add some loose parts to your lightbox to explore sun loose art by exploring coloured tangrams, glass beads and even yellow flower petals and photos of the sun.

- Make your own suncatcher by collecting flower petals and sticking these onto sticky back plastic, putting a wooden picture frame around it and hanging it outside or in the window.
- Books to explore together: *Katie and the Sunflowers* by James Mayhew, *Sun! One in a Billion* by Stacy McAnulty and *The Solstice Badger* by Robin McFadden.

Storms

- Show a video of a storm or share the story of Noah's Ark or *The Storm* by Akiko Miyakoshi and have a discussion about what children already know about storms. Record down any questions they have and use these as a starting point. Find out what wild animals do when there is a storm. Can you build a den inside? Work together as a group to make your own storm cloud and hang it up.
- Go outside after a storm and take a look for storm damage, looking for fallen branches, rubbish blown out of the bin or damage to the environment.
- Set up a stormy beach small world scene.
- Create a stormy weather playdough tray with white pom poms, blue glass beads and yellow wool for lightning.
- Make rainmakers using re-cycled yoghurt pots and fill with beads, couscous or dried rice. Create your own music and sing I hear thunder or I'm singing in the rain.
- Collect some rain outside in a pot and see if you can paint with the rain.
- Add rainy day clothes and props to your dramatic play centre.
- Books to explore together: *The Storm Whale* by Benji Davies, *Thunder Cake* by Patricia Polacco and *The Storm* by Akiko Miyakos.

Snow

- Catch snowflakes on your mitten or on a black cloth and try to draw them before they melt. Take a look at these under the microscope. What happens to it when brought inside?
- Notice the various patterns of snow sculpting that are formed by the wind drifting the snow. Can you spot any animal tracks?
- Set up a snowflake loose parts provocation with mirrored base boards, blue glass gems, blue and white buttons, snowflake pattern cards, white beads and cotton and bamboo cotton buds.
- Collect some snow and put it in a container in the freezer. Get this out in the warmer months to add curiosity.

- Display snowflake decorations on the lightbox and project paper dollies onto a blank wall to add enchantment or play a snowstorm on the smartboard.
- Books to explore together: *The Story of Snow: The Science of Winter's Wonder* by Mark Cassino, *Snow in the Garden: A First Book of Christmas* by Shirley Hughes, *One Snowy Night* (*A Tale from Percy's Park*) by Nick Butterwort and *Snowballs* (*Rise and Shine*) by Lois Ehlert.

Chapter seventeen

BRINGING NATURE INSIDE

Having real plants and foliage in your environment has lots of positive benefits, including boosting your mood, productivity, concentration and creativity. They also help to reduce your stress, fatigue and prevent sore throats and colds. This is due to the way they clean indoor air by absorbing toxins, increasing humidity and producing oxygen. In this chapter we will audit your environment for nature opportunities and share examples of how settings I have worked with have made changes and the positive impact it's had.

Creating a nature shelf

Why not create a very special home to treasure and appreciate all your lovely natural finds? A little space on a shelf will be just perfect, a collection in a shoebox or even a display in the middle of your dining table. It's a wonderful way to bring the connection with the great outdoors into your home and to celebrate the season. It can be something very simple found on a walk like a pinecone, a rock, flowers from the garden or a feather. My member Claire has also brought nature into her space by creating a seasonal curiosity box.

DOI: 10.4324/9781003189954-22

I like to add our drawings and paintings of the natural find too or a question on some card we've been curious about. If you have the space you can maybe add some beautiful decorations you find of nature or a postcard that lights you up.

Some things to collect over December might be:

- Pinecones
- Off cuttings from your Christmas tree
- Twigs labelled from different trees
- Holly leaves and berries
- Fluffy white seed heads of Old Man's Beard
- Orange seeds of spindle trees
- Bark from the tree
- Hazel catkins
- Ivy and winter jasmine

When the nature shelf is positioned in a space that parents can also see it helps to create a connection between home and school as well.

Here is a collection of ideas you could enhance your shelf with:

- Books
- Photographs
- Magnifying glasses
- Sketch pads
- Art materials
- Child voice cards
- Natural objects
- Collectors pots
- Cameras
- Spotter sheets
- Vases and jam jars filled with seasonal flowers
- Small world

Activity

Create a plan of how you can set up a seasonal nature space inside. Here are some prompts to support you:

- Where will it be located?
- Will parents be able to see it?
- What are the key resources you'll use?
- How will children be able to contribute to it?
- How often will you change it?

Add plants

The NASA clean air study shows that adding plants to your indoor space is great for purifying the air. There are many to choose from – money plants, cacti, palms, spider plants – that can all have great impact, but always research those that are safe around children.

You could also involve the children in planting up window boxes with bulbs such as Muscari, Crocosmia and Alliums. Planting alliums is great for the bees and also they create a beautiful display of colour in late spring.

After a storm why not go on the hunt for some fallen tree branches that you can bring back and place in your provision. They could be suspended from your ceiling and draped in fairy lights to give a wonderful hygge glow.

Why not create a terrarium in a clear fish tank by filling the tank with layers of gravel, sand, and soil and plant in some mosses and ferns. Having a mini eco-system in your classroom allows young children to explore changes.

Lastly, plant seeds of fast-growing vines such as beans and sweet peas inside that you can then move outside as they begin to get bigger. You can also try growing some cress seeds and enjoy cress sandwiches once they've grown enough.

Loose parts

Natural loose parts can make great open-ended resources that give children the connection with nature as they work actively with them. They can be added throughout your areas of provision like the playdough for example where children can explore texture and pattern. Here is a list of some of my favourites to include:

- Pinecones
- Leaves
- Sticks
- Logs
- Tree cookies
- Water
- Herbs
- Slices of dried fruit
- Pegs
- Dried flowers
- Flower heads
- Seeds
- Flower petals
- Shells of different sizes and shapes
- Sea glass
- Driftwood
- Feathers

(Don't take anything that is alive or could be an animal home and don't take pebbles away from the beach.)

For my member Alex Smith, a reception teacher based in Central London, she realised from growing up and going to school in central London and now teaching in central London the sheer lack of outdoor learning opportunities there are.

> I began incorporating natural materials into the different areas of my provision: adding the natural world within Maths and in loose part play. The children are also invited to add collected items to the nature treasures box that then get added to our loose parts trolley.
>
> (Alex Smith, reception teacher)

Main takeaways from Part 4

- We have become an indoor generation and we can learn from research that this isn't good for our health and wellbeing.
- Instead of dreading the rain or the bad weather in the winter we must learn to embrace it and celebrate the opportunities it brings.
- The outdoors offers a richness that we can't find inside and so when we go into nature, we don't need a prior agenda, we just need to learn to be in that moment. Then the learning will naturally happen.

SUMMARY OF BOOK

If you can take one thing from my book I want you to hold on to it's to slow down. When you do this you're calmer, you feel happier, you're not rushing from one thing to the next and you have room to just breathe. No one likes to feel as though their hectic and busyness is not a sign of success.

When we slow down and appreciate the simple moments in life we model to the children that we work with that this is OK.

In such a fast-paced world perhaps slowing down should be an important life skill to learn.

Laura from Stone Hen Childcare reflects on how the hygge journey has impacted her team and the practice that they do.

> Discovering "Hygge in the Early Years" dramatically impacted the underpinning ethos of our early years provision, deeply influencing and improving the practice of my professional team. The concept of hygge provided us with a beautiful insight into cross-cultural perspectives, which we could then apply and adapt into our everyday practice. We were able to implement this concept of professional wellbeing throughout a variety of ways to support not only the children, their families, and the wider community; but to rediscover the joy and true spirit of what it means to be an early years teacher.
>
> Embracing a love-based leadership approach, provides us with more sincere inter-professional relationships, liberates the practitioners creative flow, and empowers all our staff to be leaders of learning. Not just facilitating high quality learning only for the children and families, but with more enthusiasm and curiosity within their own professional development journey too. Hygge reminded us of the joy and calm that can be discovered within even the smallest of moments or experiences. Although we are not a Danish provision, we have

been able to integrate and adapt such beautiful values to that of our own unique community and landscapes. We as a united team of children and professionals are mindful of the present moment, more aware of our own self-care and emotional intelligence, and living life with a smile each day.

(Laura Brothwell, Stone Hen Childcare)

BIBLIOGRAPHY

Alexander, J. (2016). *Hygge: The Danish Art of Being in the Moment*. Available at: https://www.thelocal.dk/20160426/hygge-danish-being-in-the-moment (accessed 22 March 2021).

Archer, S. (2011). *The Happiness Advantage: The Seven Principles of Positive Psychology that Fuel Success and Performance at Work*. London: Virgin Books.

Barrable, A., and Arvanitis, A. (2019). Flourishing in the forest: Looking at Forest School through a self-determination theory lens. *Journal of Outdoor and Environmental Education, 22*, 39–55. Available at: https://doi.org/10.1007/s42322-018-0018-5 (accessed 19 February 2021).

Beatty, B. (2000). "The letter killeth": Americanization and multicultural education in kindergartens in the United States, 1856–1920. In *Kindergartens and Cultures: The Global Diffusion of an Idea*, edited by Roberta Woolons, 42–58. New Haven, CT: Yale University Press.

Brits, L. T. (2016). *The Book of Hygge: The Danish Art of Living Well, Ebury Press*. London: Penguin Random House UK.

Brosterman, N. (1997). *Inventing Kindergarten*. New York: Harry N. Abrams, Inc.

Bruce, T. (2005). *Early Childhood Education*. London: Hodder Education.

Bucholz, J. L., and Sheffler, J. L. (2009). Creating a warm and inclusive classroom environment: Planning for all children to feel welcome. *Electronic Journal for Inclusive Education, 2*(4). Available at: http://corescholar.libraries.wright.edu/cgi/viewcontent.cgi?article=1102&context=ejie (accessed 22 March 2021).

Clay, R. A. (2004). No more Mickey Mouse design: Child's environments require unique considerations. In *ASID ICON*, 43–47.

Dam, H., Jakobsen, K., and Mellerup, E. (1998). Prevalence of winter depression in Denmark. *Acta Psychiatrica Scandinavica, 97*(1), 1–4. doi: 10.1111/j.1600-0447.1998.tb09954.x. PMID: 9504695. Available at: https://pubmed.ncbi.nlm.nih.gov/9504695/ (accessed 4 February 2021).

Dorman, J. and Aldridge, J., and Fraser, B. (2006). Using students' assessment of classroom environment to develop a typology of secondary school classrooms. *International Education Journal*, 7(7), 906–915. Available at: https://www.researchgate.net/publication/242144046_Using_students'_assessment_of_classroom_environment_to_develop_a_typology_of_secondary_school_classrooms (accessed 23 February 2021).

Fadiga, L., Fogassi, L., Pavesi, G., and Rizzolatti, G. (1995). Motor facilitation during action observation: A magnetic stimulation study. *Journal of Neurophysiology, 73*, 2608–2611. Available at: https://citeseerx.ist.psu.edu/viewdoc/download?doi=10.1.1.299.4524&rep=rep1&type=pdf (accessed 23 April 2021).

Frank, M. G., and Gilovich, T. (1988). The dark side of self- and social perception: Black uniforms and aggression in professional sports. *Journal of Personality and Social Psychology, 54*(1), 74–85. doi: 10.1037//0022-3514.54.1.74. PMID: 3346809.

Freed, J., and Parsons, L. (1997). *Right-Brained Children in a Left-Brained World*. New York: Fireside.

Furuyashiki, A., Tabuchi, K., Norikoshi, K., Kobayashi, T., and Oriyama, S. (2019). A comparative study of the physiological and psychological effects of forest bathing (Shinrin-yoku) on working age people with and without depressive tendencies. *Environmental Health and Preventive Medicine, 24*(1), 46. doi: 10.1186/s12199-019-0800-1. PMID: 31228960; PMCID: PMC6589172.

Garcia, H. (2017). *Ikigai: Tha Japanese Secret to a Long and Happy Life*. London: Hutchinson.

Goethe W. (1810). *Theory of Colors*. London: Frank Cass.

Haig, M. (2015). *Reasons to Stay Alive*. Edinburgh: Canongate Books Ltd.

Haig, M. (2021). *The Midnight Library*. Edinburgh: Canongate Books Ltd.

Mark, G., Gudith, D., and Klocke, U. (2008). The cost of interrupted work: More speed and stress. In Proceedings of the SIGCHI Conference on Human Factors in Computing Systems (CHI '08). Association for Computing Machinery, New York, 107–110. Available at: https://doi.org/10.1145/1357054.1357072 (accessed 5 March 2021).

McCarty, J. (1999). The effects of school uniforms on student behavior and perceptions in an Urban Middle School. PhD dissertation, Old Dominion University, DOI: 10.25777/q2dm-tf68 Available at: https://digitalcommons.odu.edu/urbanservices_education_etds/40 (accessed 5 March 2021).

Melrose S. (2015). Seasonal affective disorder: An overview of assessment and treatment approaches. *Depression Research and Treatment, 2015*, 178564. doi:10.1155/2015/178564

Ministry of Foreign Affairs of Denmark (2021) *Working in Denmark: Work-life Balance*. Available at: https://denmark.dk/society-and-business/work-life-balance#:~:text=Danes%20are%20some%20of%20Europe's,every%20desk%20will%20be%20empty (accessed 6 January 2021).

Myler, P. A., Fantacone, T. A., and Merritt, E. T. (2003). Eliminating distractions: The educational needs of autistic children challenge ordinary approaches to school design. *Journal of Family & Consumer Sciences Education, 29*(1), 313–317. Available at: https://www.natefacs.org/Pages/v29no1/v29no1Gaines.pdf (accessed 14 March 2021).

NHS. (2021). *Stress: Every-Mind-Matters*. Available at: https://www.nhs.uk/every-mind-matters/mental-health-issues/stress/#:~:text=Support%20for%20stress-,What%20is%20stress%3F,home%2C%20work%20and%20family%20life (accessed 1 March 2021).

Palmer, S. (2007). *Toxic Childhood: How The Modern World Is Damaging Our Children and What We Can Do About It*. London: Orion Books.

Preschool Learning Alliance. (2018). *Minds Matter The Impact of Working in the Early Years Sector on Practitioners' Mental Health and Wellbeing*. Available at: https://www.eyalliance.org.uk/sites/default/files/minds_matter_report_pre-school_learning_alliance.pdf (accessed 2 January 2021).

Robson, D. (2010). *The Five Pillars of Happiness: Your New Life: Step by Step (Wellbeing)*. London: Wizard Publishing.

Schindler, I., Hosoya, G., Menninghaus, W., Beermann, U., Wagner, V., Eid, M., and Scherer, K. R. (2017). Measuring aesthetic emotions: A review of the literature and a new assessment tool. *PLoS*

One, *5;12*(6), e0178899. Available at: https://journals.plos.org/plosone/article?id=10.1371/journal.pone.0178899 (accessed 26 January 2021).

Seligman, M. E., Steen, T. A., Park, N., and Peterson, C. (2005). Positive psychology progress: Empirical validation of interventions. *American Psychologist*, *60*(5), 410–421.

Siraj-Blatchford, I., and Manni, L. (2004). *Good Question*. Available at: https://www.nurseryworld.co.uk/news/article/good-question (accessed 17 March 2021).

Siraj-Blatchford, I., Sylva, K., Muttock, S., Gilden, R., and Bell, D. (2002). *Researching Effective Pedagogy in the Early Years*.

Soldat, A. S., Sinclair, R. C., and Mark, M. M. (1997). Color as an environmental processing cue: External affective cues can directly affect processing strategy without affecting mood. *Social Cognition*, *15*(1), 55–71. Available at: https://doi.org/10.1521/soco.1997.15.1.55 (accessed 21 Febraury 2021).

Stokes, S. (under contract with CESA 7 and funded by a discretionary grant from the Wisconsin Department of Public Instruction). (2003). Structured teaching: Strategies for supporting students with autism? Available at: https://www.cesa7.k12.wi.us/sped/autism/structured/str10.htm (accessed 3 January 2021).

Stothart, C., Mitchum, A., and Yehnert, C. (2015). The attentional cost of receiving a cell phone notification. *Journal of Experimental Psychology: Human Perception and Performance*, *41*(4), 893–897. Available at: https://doi.org/10.1037/xhp0000100 (accessed 29 March 2021).

Sylva, K., Melhuish, E., Sammons, P., Siraj, I., and Taggart, B. (2004). The effective provision of pre-school education (EPPE) project technical paper 12: Findings from pre-school to end of key stage 1. The Final Report – Effective Pre-School Education.

Trachtenberg, F. L., Haas, E. A., Kinney, H. C., Stanley, C., and Krous, H. F. (2012). Risk factor changes for sudden infant death syndrome after initiation of Back-to-Sleep campaign. *Pediatrics*, *129*, 630–638. Published online 26 March 2012. Available at: http://pediatrics.aappublications.org/content/early/2012/03/21/peds.2011-1419.abstract (accessed 15 March 2021).

Wiking, M. (2016). *The Little Book of Hygge*. London: Penguin Life.

Williams-Siegfredsen, J. (2011). *Understanding the Danish Forest School Approach: Early Years Education in Practice*. Abingdon: Routledge.

Wright, A. (1998). *The Beginner's Guide to Colour Psychology*. London: Colour Affects.

INDEX